"In order for any teenager to dream, they must have good role models to follow. *Be Committed. Get Admitted!* offers the perfect balance of good practical tips and a hearty dose of encouragement. Students no longer have to wait until their junior year to get the information they need to plan and prepare for a successful college application process."

Jack Canfield
Coauthor of the *Chicken Soup for the Soul*® series and *The Success Principles™: How to Get from Where You Are to Where You Want to Be*

"Dr. Colón combines practical tips with candid insights into the college admission process for students from across the academic spectrum. She provides actionable advice for students that makes them feel confident and inspired about applying to college. Parents will feel like insiders, while teens walk away feeling prepared, and ready for a stress-free senior year! I entrusted my son to Dr. Dr. Colón's care for the application advice and support he needed."

Dr. Yvonne Romero da Silva
Vice President of Enrollment, Rice University

"*Be Committed. Get Admitted!* is an important guidebook for all families, especially for first generation students and families of color. I appreciate Dr. Colón's personal and enlightening story telling style. She gives it to you straight, within the context of her Latina roots. Navigating the college search process has never been easy for most families, but this book will empower you to make better decisions throughout high school."

Rodney Morrison
Vice President for Enrollment Management, University of Delaware

D1571917

"Cynthia Colón's work in admissions assisted many students to reach their dreams and now she is taking that experience and desire to give back in writing *Be Committed. Get Admitted!* Cynthia "walks the talk" and shares "words of wisdom" gleaned from her experiences in an easy to read and edifying book for teens aspiring to reach their college dreams and beyond."

Dr. Cynthia Cherrey
Former Vice President for Campus Life, Princeton University
Former Vice President for Student Affairs, Tulane University
International Leadership Association President and CEO

"Dr. Cynthia Colón is a leading voice and has so much information to share! She gives candid advice and has such a record of success working with students and families in the college search process. Whether you are a student, a parent, or perhaps a college advisor, you will want to have Dr. Colón's latest book on your bookshelf."

Thomas P. Rock, Ed.D.
Vice Provost for Student Affairs, Teachers College, Columbia University

---

"What I love about Dr. Colón's book, *Be Committed. Get Admitted!*, is how relatable it is for any and every college bound teen. The students highlighted in the book come from public and private schools and hail from big city to small town America. Whether you are third generation or first generation (like me) to college, this book is a must read."

Marcela Mejia-Martinez
Assistant VP of Admission, Chapman University

"Chock-full of information about managing the college search, *Be Committed. Get Admitted!* encourages students to take hold of and purposefully shape their high school years. Through genuine and engaging anecdotes, and many years of experience as an educator, Dr. Colón offers high school students and families the know-how needed to lay the groundwork for applying to college."

Art D. Rodriguez
VP and Dean of Admission and Financial Aid, Carleton College
Former Dean of Admission & Financial Aid, Vassar College

"As a prominent voice in the world of college admission, Dr. Cynthia Colón's advice to high school students is spot on! Every student who dreams of going to college should read this book – it's funny, entertaining and informative. After reading *Be Committed. Get Admitted!*, I have no doubt students and parents will be begging her for even more words of wisdom!"

Sarah Gallagher Dvorak
Director of Admission at Saint Mary's College in Notre Dame, IN

"Working in Student Affairs, I interact with hundreds of students and families each year as they are making their final decisions about whether to attend our university, and I can see that for many, they still don't have a clear strategy about how to make that choice. Dr. Colón's book will help students map their priorities well in advance of that deadline for making this major decision. While the book helps students approach the college admission process intentionally, I like that *Be Committed. Get Admitted!* encourages students to be reflective and genuine, rather than simply providing a checklist to follow."

Jayne E. Brownell, Ed.D.
Vice President for Student Affairs, Miami University (OH)

"*Be Committed. Get Admitted!* is the book every family should have on their bookshelf. Dr. Colon comes across as the perfect blend of pushy parent and encouraging aunt. The tales are relatable to students of all backgrounds and talents. Whether you are looking for helpful college application tips or wanting to gain insider information on the college application process, this book is for you!"

Kelsey Kaplan
Assistant Director for First Year Recruitment, UNLV

"Lynwood Unified is committed to having 100% of our seniors apply to college. Dr. Colon's easy-to-follow methods and strategies give our students confidence to apply, courage to share their stories, and assurance that applying to the right colleges will ensure multiple "Yes" letters."

Shawn Dinkins, Ed.D.
Deputy Superintendent, Lynwood Unified School District

"Cynthia and I share a passion for ensuring that students from all backgrounds have an equal opportunity to access top colleges. *Be Committed. Get Admitted!* offers the very tips and strategies I shared as an admission officer at Vassar College and Columbia University. This book helps to close the education and information gap between private and public school students."

Tamar Adegbile
Director of Student Wellbeing and College Counseling, The Avenues School
Former Admission Officer: Vassar College, Columbia University

"Dr. Colón has recently partnered with my school, WISH Academy High School and so far the presentations and accompanying information has proven invaluable to my students and their parents. This journey with Dr. Colón has thus far been highly collaborative, insightful and has shown me just how much has changed since I navigated the college admissions process."

Kimberly Y. Johnson, Ed.D.
Principal, WISH Community and Academy Schools

"This newest edition of Dr. Colón's book will demystify the process of selective college admissions in an entertaining way, featuring stories of real teens and their families and how they successfully navigated the college process to achieve their dreams. Dr. Colón's outlines a four-year process, step by step. Follow along from curricular choices, creating a balanced list of colleges, building a resume, to telling a distinctive story in your essay, and ultimately receiving the "We want YOU!" message from several colleges on your list.

Vanna Cairns
Former Upper School Dean, Harvard-Westlake School

"Dr. C presented to our South Pasadena PTSA and parents raved about the simplicity and practicality of the college admission lessons in her book. The tales hit home for the average student to the overachiever. *Be Committed. Get Admitted!* is the perfect book for every parent and teen to read together."

Stacey Petersen
Executive Director www.SPEF4kids.org

"Being "student-centered" in one's counseling and admission practices is the gold standard in my opinion, and that of many thought leaders and reformers in the field. Dr. Colón is a natural at this; it is weaved into the personal and professional fiber of her being. The stories and anecdotes contained in *Be Committed. Get Admitted!* are a testament to this and the expertise she brings to the field of college counseling."

Philip "PJ" Petrone
Co-Director of College Counseling and Director of SAILL - Marymount High School, Los Angeles

---

"Youth across the nation need a cheerleader and guide to help them build their high school college application over four years. Dr. Cynthia Colón provides *Be Committed. Get Admitted!* in a fun and tangible format. As a first generation college graduate and a former guidance counselor, she offers vulnerability, transparency and veracity about the college admission process. The reader can hear Dr. Colón cheering emphatically through the words on the pages for youth to find their passion and their own leadership voice on this journey to achieve their own "impossible" dream."

Dr. Erin Brunner Richison
Area Superintendent at San Diego Unified School District

"Dr. Colón draws on her rich professional experience to deliver a dynamic guidebook to help navigate what at times can be a daunting and Byzantine experience for high school students and their families. Possessing the credibility and unique perspective of someone who has spent time as both a high school college counselor as well as an admissions officer in one of the most selective institutions in higher education, *Be Committed. Get Admitted!* stands as a powerful roadmap that should be required reading for all students who are planning on going to college, but are just unsure how to get there."

Mr. Casey Yeazel
Chief of Staff, Los Angeles Archdiocese Department of Catholic Schools

As a thank you gift from me, download your sample packet:

10 WINNING COLLEGE ESSAYS
TO GET YOU STARTED!

**SCAN THE QR CODE
AND BECOME A PRO AT
GETTING ADMITTED!**

BE COMMITTED.

Get Admitted!

7 STEPS TO COLLEGE ADMISSION SUCCESS

© DR. CYNTHIA COLÓN

BE COMMITTED.
GET ADMITTED.

Cover Design & Layout by Margaret Cogswell Designs
Printed in the United States of America

ISBN: 979-8-9880722-0-1

Dedicated to
my biggest cheerleaders
and grandest believers,
Mom and Dad.

YOUR 7 STEP GRAND PLAN

Shoot for the Moon, but make a plan to get there.

Ninety percent of your college application happens before senior year.
Don't put off for next year what you can do now.

Look up, look out, and look forward to trying everything!

Do what is right. Find your inner leader. Utilize your passion.
Leave a legacy.

INTRODUCTION:

Every teen needs a mentor. Not just any mentor, the right mentor.

I found myself at one of the oldest colleges in the country and had access to the Ivy League and other Sister schools. As a young woman in my 20s—I had no idea what this meant, how significant this would be, and what I would discover about myself and the college admissions process. This is my story.

I grew up with 14 Tíos and Tías (uncles and aunts) who had advice for just about every topic, except, how to get admitted to college. My mother didn't know how to help me, but she was determined to see me achieve my dreams. She drove me in the brown Oldsmobile up the 110 freeway to meet with Mr. Vargas. It was Mr. Vargas who was the mentor I needed. After that meeting, I became committed to getting admitted. USC became my sandbox for four years and after graduating from my dream college, I headed east for graduate school at Teachers College, Columbia University. My internship at Barnard College made me uniquely attractive to snag an interview and was hired at one of the oldest colleges in the country. Within a couple years, I switched departments for the glamorous (or so I thought) traveling life of an Admission Officer. I had no idea what I would discover.

Working as an Admission Officer at Vassar gave me access to other admission officers at Ivy League and Sister institutions. At the young age of 26, I was being mentored by folks from the 14 most elite colleges in the country. I quickly realized that the students at these 14 colleges were a whole other caliber of student.

Once I began recruiting students for Vassar I visited private high schools across the country and saw for myself just how ill prepared I was when I left my public high school in comparison to private school students. I drove up to campuses with a guard gate and behind that gate were brick layered buildings, manicured landscaping, students taking Mandarin in elementary school, high school classrooms with less than 15 students per class, and every AP course on the menu. In addition to the access and exposure these students had daily, at the most elite high schools they also hosted an annual case studies event, in which admission folks like myself walked the parents and students through the anatomy of successful applications. They saw first hand the college admission process. An advantage not offered 95% of students across the country.

To say these students were born to earn a place at a top 100 college is an understatement.

More than anything, I understood this one fact: the elite private school students had access to parents, teachers, coaches, and other peers who had gone before them, a plethora of mentors. I don't know about you, but I love to follow a plan, a path, a formula that has already been proven to work, and there inside those brick layered buildings were all the answers.

I began taking notes everywhere I went.

I was on it. I was determined to crack the code. I studied every high school I went to, every student I met. I asked questions of every counselor who would answer—and at night I would record my findings in my journal. I became an anthropologist studying student behavior and a sociologist of habits of the families they belonged to.

I became obsessed with the college admission process.

My obsession took me to the elite girls school, Marymount HS in Los Angeles. They were looking to increase the profile of where the girls got admitted to college. This is where I put my findings into action and shared the strategies and wisdom I had gained with my private school students. The percent of students admitted to top 100 colleges began to rise, in spite of an increasing high demand with limited supply of admission spots available. Within just two years the girls were admitted to Duke, Brown, Harvard, Stanford, Princeton, Yale, and the list went on.

When I say I became obsessed, I mean it.

It's been nearly 25 years since I first sat on the beaches of Miami, took notes on the Riverwalk in San Antonio, or jotted down a tip or strategy I needed to communicate. I was on a mission then and even more now to become the pocket mentor, aka the "Mr. Vargas," that millions of students need each and every year. The 30 tales found in that book are real life stories, candid examples, and practical to-dos to help make YOUR dream come true. The book was designed to give every teenager (and family), no matter their background, the exact knowledge, access, and exposure to opportunities not always available to ALL college bound teens. The adults featured are meant to be mentors, and the highlighted students serve as role models, and I hope, with all my heart, that I can serve as your biggest cheerleader!

I do not purport to have all the answers; I am a product of my own journey and life lessons. What I offer is a 7 Step Plan with tales to apply to your own journey. Each story is divided into three easy-to-read parts:

TIP

This recommendation comes from wearing my college counseling hat. I am the voice of your counselor, advisor, and mentor all in one.

TALE

Many students I have met from around the country have inspired these mini-dramas I call tales. Each tale offers a unique story inspired by real students. Some tales are from my own high school experience, where I was known as Cyndie. Others are from my encounters at Marymount High School, where I was known as Ms. Colón. The tales with Vassar College as the backdrop, I was simply known as Cynthia. The recounted stories from Dr. Colón are those from my days as principal at St. Bernard High School. And the most recent tales are students who have taken courses like Dream College Academy (DCA) and/or College Essay Bootcamp. Those students know me as Dr. C.

TRUTH

This section is my candid advice as a veteran college admission officer. I offer the truth as my advice on what you can take away from the tale and a reminder of what you do have control over in the college admission process. In many cases I offer practical "To dos" at the end.

Be Committed. Get Admitted! 7 Steps To College Admission Success is laid out in seven chapters, each designed to offer a specific plan on how you can manage this seemingly unwieldy process. While I recommend reading them in order, it is easy to go through the table of contents and find a tip you may need for motivation today. No worries and no judgment. You do you. It's all about you!

CHAPTER 1: Your Four-Year Plan

Whether you are the first in your family to attend college, have siblings in college, or your parents graduated from an Ivy League institution, applying to college is new to YOU. Believe it or not, ninety percent of the college application happens before senior year. This chapter offers two key rules: get a mentor and make a plan.

CHAPTER 2: Your Academic Plan

As a college bound teen, you are applying from one academic institution to another. That said, you need to get your Academic Qualities (AQs) in order. This chapter reveals the five academic food groups and answers the age-old question, "Is it better to get an A in a regular course, or a B in an honors or AP course?"

CHAPTER 3: Your Resume Plan

Whether your interests lie in clubs, service, athletics, performing arts, or competitive organizations, the message here is to get involved and do something. While your AQs will get your foot in the door, students need to consider their Personal Qualities (PQs). And while you do not have to fill up your "dance card" with a litany of clubs, this chapter is a reminder that interested students make for interesting applicants.

CHAPTER 4: Your Leadership Plan

If you are a natural leader and/or planning to apply to top 100 colleges, this chapter is for you. Colleges are in search of all types of leaders, and top colleges look for those who leave an impact. This chapter offers examples of how real students found what I call their "Coolness Factor."

CHAPTER 5: Your Self-Improvement Plan

This is my favorite chapter, as I believe failure is the perfect ingredient needed for any teen to find the courage necessary to push forward and ultimately, succeed. Chapter 5 is a reminder of just how amazing you are and how much control you have in this process.

CHAPTER 6: Your Senior Year Plan

If you've followed the plan, by September of senior year, ninety percent of the heavy lifting is over. All that is left to do is put all those puzzle pieces together, complete the forms, and hit submit. This chapter offers a step-by-step process for building your list of colleges, how to choose your essay topic, how to ask for teacher letters of recommendation, and how to relieve stress while you wait.

CHAPTER 7: Your New Plan Awaits

This chapter is an homage to the month of April that comes in senior year. I offer a variety of mini-dramas highlighting the joy, fear, disappointment, worry, confusion, and elation that comes with receiving Red, Yellow, and Green (deny, waitlist, admit) admission decisions. I say, go celebrate the courage you had to apply and the sublime feeling of every victorious "Yes!"

Oh and one last thing…

My hope is that you will not only read *Be Committed. Get Admitted! 7 Steps To College Admission Success*, but go back and reference the bigger ideas and lessons that somehow shifted something inside you when you first read each tale. Every stage of your life journey is different, but everyone needs a mentor and cheerleader along the way. Keep this book handy for the next time you are in need of a "pocket mentor." This book will come in handy as you navigate through college, apply for internships or scholarships, and when you begin job and career hunting.

High school represents the most formidable years of your life. You will achieve great things, you will fail, you will make great choices and you will make mistakes. You will form lasting friendships, you will be disappointed, you will find your confidence, and you will often doubt yourself. You will fall in love, you will have your heart broken, and you will find yourself because of these events. Balancing all of the above, while also having to think about your future, is a lot to ask of any teenager. It can be overwhelming, I know. But, I promise, nothing about the college admission process is impossible with a role model or mentor by your side. If you haven't found one yet, let me do the honors through your process, or until you find that adult who believes in you just as much (or more) as I do!

Now, let's get to it!

DR. CYNTHIA COLÓN

CHAPTER 1

YOUR 4-YEAR PLAN

CHAPTER 1:
Introduction

While I was on the road recruiting for Vassar College in Florida, Texas, Kansas, Minnesota, and California one lesson became crystal clear to me: every private school student had a 4-year plan. They didn't necessarily come up with this plan on their own; what I'm saying is that the school leaders, counselors, and the adults at each school had a plan, a system, and a college-going culture that far preceded their arrival.

When I interviewed my mother, Lydia Franco, as the first guest on my podcast, she had one message to share with parents. As an immigrant child herself, her mother discouraged her from accepting a place at one of the two colleges she had been admitted to, and yet somehow, my mother got all three of her daughters admitted and enrolled in college. How? My mother's belief is simple: Remove the word "If" from your vocabulary and replace it with, "When." This is what I call the "When-Win" situation.

My mother's belief is simple: Remove the word "If" from your vocabulary and replace it with, "When." This is what I call the "When-Win" situation.

"When I go to college, When I get an A on that exam, When I land the audition, When I win that competition…" I can go on, but you get the idea. As a teenager, I did not realize that that simple word that my mother used with me (all day everyday) meant that I never questioned whether or not I would attend college, but rather, my only question was where.

Whether you are in 8th grade or about to begin your college applications now, I am proud of you. The fact that you are reading this book tells me all I need to know about you. YOU have made a decision that WHEN you apply to college, you will be ready!

Ok, now that you have the mindset that you will apply, get admitted, and enroll, now you need a plan. In this chapter you will learn how to take action, meet your counselor, how to find a mentor, and what you need to do to backwards engineer your academic and leadership plan.

Buckle up and hear the candid lessons from these real students who are just like YOU!

Let's get to it!

| TIP #1 | Take Action. Ask For Help. |

TALE:
The Zoom Where It Happened.

While the world dealt with a global pandemic, tonight, nothing seemed to stand in the way of the hopes and dreams of 30 high school students. The summer online Dream College Academy (DCA) course invited students to meet weekly for a seven-week comprehensive college counseling curriculum. On this Thursday night we had our usual mix of students; Malik, from Virginia, Cosette from Maryland, Jalyn and Ryan from Texas, Caroline from Georgia, Janah from Illinois, and Ethan and Miles from California.

Week one was about mindset. "Dreamers" had to create vision boards and post them to the FB group. "Would anyone like to share their big hairy goal in life," addressing a screen full of students was becoming less awkward as students knew how and when to mute and unmute themselves. "I want to go to USC," Ethan broke the silence. Ryan unmuted and shared, "I want to play professional baseball." And with that, the flood gates opened. Jalyn was writing a children's book, Caroline and Malik were hoping to find clarity throughout the course, Miles planned to major in engineering or computer science. Cosette waited her turn until and then shared with pride, "I want to work for Disney." Wow, I thought! With each share out the students unmuted as I counted to three and did a ONE Clap. Zoom wasn't the best at synchronizing those One Claps, but they each felt the praise nonetheless.

We were just about out of time, but I knew Janah had her hand raised for some time now, she would be the last one I called on tonight. With the bubble gum pink background, Janah sat straight up in her bedroom in Chicago and announced, "I want to be the President." Without hesitation, I knew what she meant. Janah didn't say she wanted to be President, she said THE President. "Janah, just so we are all clear, you mean you want to be the President of the United States?" A simple, "Yes," followed and in that moment my nickname for her became, "Little POTUS."

In just one week, these students were off to the races. With the weeks that followed, "How to calculate your GPA," "How to beef up your resume," "How to find a major and create your college list," "How to write the essay," "How to ask for letters of recommendation," our Dreamers showed up on Zoom ready with questions, encouragement and a willingness to learn from each other. We learned that Malik was the youngest, as a rising sophomore, Malik had big dreams and his mother thought DCA was perfect to get him started early. Caroline's mom had no idea how to help her daughter navigate through the college admission process, so she called me and eventually signed her up for DCA and essay camp. This group became a family, a village of cheerleaders.

Cosette quickly became a leader. She had been through the college admission process twice before, once as a senior in high school, followed by one more round as a hopeful transfer. She was unsuccessful both times with zero acceptances to show for. Yes, I said zero. Cosette was undeterred, and it was her mother who was determined to help Cosette fulfill her dream of attending college. Cosette watched every module, every video, and showed up to every Zoom session with one goal in mind: ASK QUESTIONS. As chance would have it, Week FOUR, one of our guests worked for Disney. Before the end of that session, Cosette had a plan. She followed up with an email, Annie then connected her with someone from animation, and later that summer Cosette had an hour-long meeting with an animator from Disney.

Janah played the slow and steady game. Each week she'd brighten up our evening with her bubble gum pink walls at home. She studied every guest and knew what to ask and continued to encourage her fellow Dreamers. At the end of the summer, Janah and her mother requested a meeting with me. I knew her big dream and Janah's mom knew that getting accepted to the best college possible would get Janah closer to that goal. From that moment on, Little POTUS and I became a team.

TRUTH

I believe every dream is worth pursuing. The moment the Dreamers shared it out loud with each other, they were manifesting their dreams. Behind every dream is a teenager who is willing to put in the work to make that dream a reality. Each and every one of these Dreamers were determined to make it happen. By the end of this book, you will learn what happened to Cosette and Janah.

The truth is, you cannot do it alone. Step one in taking action is asking for help. Asking for help is not easy, but those who do ask discover a village of cheerleaders just waiting to be of service.

Teachers, counselors, coaches, mentors, community leaders all want to help YOU. I promise. Trust that they have even a tiny piece of advice to offer that will make your college admission journey that *Behind every dream is a teenager who is willing to put in the work to make that dream a reality.* much easier. Teenagers are not supposed to know how to do this because you've never done it before. My biggest advice: Don't try this alone.

To help you ease into this process, I'll give you a few quick and actionable To Dos:

MUST DOS:

1 – Get an email that you will use only for college admissions. Having a separate email will make your life much easier and you can ask mom and dad to help with opening and keeping up with all that "love" mail.

2 – Go meet your school counselor if you haven't already. S/he is the key to your overall academic success and college "Yes!"

SHOULD DOS:

1 – Get signed up for college newsletters. My favorite piece of advice from Coach Vince: "The first time a college hears from you should not be when you submit your application in senior year." Get on their mailing list so you can get on their radar!

2 – Get a copy of your School Profile. If you Google your high school name plus the words "School Profile" it should come

up. For example, if you google, "McKinney High School School Profile," you will find a PDF of the school profile. This is the information colleges use to know and understand the context in which you come from.

COULD DO:

1 – Get a mentor. You can literally get a mentor at school who is willing to talk to you about college and advise you on what to do. Or find a podcast or YouTube Channel you like (I have both).

OK. I think five to-do items will get you moving! Take action and ask for help, that is your only job right now. Go get 'em, tiger!

| TIP #2 | Meet Your School Counselor Early and Often. |

TALE:
My Dream Weighed Less Than Eight Ounces

When I was in high school, I painted my room yellow. I watched Trojan football every Saturday, and my favorite Christmas gift was my first USC sweatshirt from my bestie, Jess. Neither of my parents had attained a college degree, but my father's love for watching the Trojan Marching Band perform on the football field at halftime, sparked my dream of becoming a cardinal-and-gold-wearing USC student. My mother attended community college and had plans of becoming a flight attendant. She was only twenty years old when my arrival stunted her dreams. While my mother knew I was infatuated with USC, it was not until November of my senior year that she understood my plight.

After working an early shift at Moffett's Family Restaurant, I was home just in time to watch the USC v. UCLA game. My sisters were with Dad for the day, and I yelled out, "Hi, Mom." I bundled up on the couch to watch the game with my cozy Trojan blanket made by Tía Irma (Tía is Spanish for aunt). Mom had no interest in sports, but she joined me at halftime.

"What's up Ladybug? You've been quiet all week," with a warm quesadilla in hand, it was a great way to get me to talk.

"Everyone at school is talking about college. Applications are due after Christmas break." I took my first bite and the cheese oozed out onto my hand.

"Yeah, and? You are applying too." I paused before responding.

"I picked up the applications for all the state schools, but the office did not have one for USC. I don't think I'll apply anyway," I stared at the television. It had been two years since my father moved out and mom was left to raise three children on a single income.

"Ladybug, I never had a chance to follow my dreams, but…"

Before she finished I asked, "But how would we pay for it?" She smiled and cried at the same time, "We will figure it out, Ladybug. We always do."

The following week was a whirlwind, and my mother was on a mission. She knew nothing about applying to college, how to pay for college, or even how to get a USC application. Mom called Tía Gloria who was a school principal who told my mother to call the counseling office at my high school and insist on an appointment right away. Mom followed the exact advice, and within 24 hours, we had an appointment. My mom may not have had a degree, but in that week, she became my superhero.

Mom took a half-day from work and met me on a Thursday after school. Mr. Vargas, whom I had only met once before, greeted my mother "Mrs. Colón, so good to meet you. We think Cyndie is doing a great job as student body president." His big smile warmed the room. Mr. Vargas offered tips for my application to USC, and more than that, he carefully explained to my mother how it was possible to pay for college with financial aid and scholarship assistance. He made sure we understood all of the deadlines, and he had an application ready for me on the way out. Mr. Vargas could make no promises, but he was encouraging nonetheless. Before I left his office, we set an appointment to meet again two weeks later.

Hindered by my own fear of not getting in, I let that application sit on the dining room table. Two weeks later, I sat in Mr. Vargas' office with nothing to report. I sat, head hung low, waiting for him to scold me as if I had ditched class. To my surprise, Mr. Vargas rolled his chair directly in front of mine. My eyes only rose up to stare back at his white beard and face with the wrinkles of a wise man. "What's the matter, Cyndie?" Like Santa Claus, Mr. Vargas whispered the words, inviting me to share why I wasn't doing anything to pursue the one Christmas gift I wanted more than anything else.

"USC is my dream school. What if I don't get in?" I tried to hold back the tears, but one escaped down my cheek.

Santa Claus waited for me to look up at him, "You'll never know unless you apply."

With that twinkle in his eye, I knew he was right. The next 24 hours was another whirlwind. I drafted my essay, completed the application, and picked up my sealed letters of recommendation from Mr. Vargas. On Tuesday after school, I walked to the post office, had the lady weigh my package, and paid for the postage.

My dream weighed less than eight ounces.

TRUTH:

Navigating the college admissions process is unwieldy for any teenager. Whether you are the first in your family to attend college, have siblings in college, or your parents graduated from an Ivy League institution, applying to college is new to YOU. And because YOU have never been through this process, I am here to help you make a plan.

The counselor is a key ingredient to your success in school and in the application process, so grab an apple or make a batch of cookies and swing by to introduce yourself.

MUST DOS:

1 – Go meet your school counselor and pronto! Do not wait to have a problem with a teacher or your schedule, and do not wait until you get in trouble because you were tardy or ditched a class (by accident). Depending on the size of your high school, it can take some time to reach a counselor and/or set up an appointment. If the office is such that you cannot just stop in, I recommend making friends with the receptionist and requesting a 15-minute appointment with your counselor for the following week.

2 – The goal as a freshman is simple: introduce yourself, ask a few questions (about schedule, college, study tips), and leave a small token of appreciation so you are remembered. That's it.

SHOULD DOS:

1 – The counselor is a key ingredient to your success in school and in the application process, so grab an apple or make a batch of cookies and swing by to introduce yourself. With this small effort s/he will remember who you are among a sea of teenagers.

COULD DO:

1 – Take note of your counselor's interests, they should be obvious in his/her office. I used to have Wonder Woman paraphernalia, college teddy bears, and colored pens all over my office. My favorite gifts were those that added to my collections. Getting to know your counselor will be the best investment you can make in yourself.

<table>
<tr><td>**TIP #3**</td><td>Find A Mentor Who Will Encourage and Push.</td></tr>
</table>

TALE:

A Dream Delayed Finally Takes Flight

Mr. Simmons worked at Los Angeles International Airport (LAX) marshaling planes in every day. Michael Simmons was a seventh grade participant when I met his father at the annual Science, Technology, Engineering, and Mathematics (STEM) Summit conference. Mr. Simmons stood at the back of the room as Michael ran over to show him the medal that bore a Viking ship. Mr. Simmons pointed at his son and whispered, "Guion," a code word only known to Michael.

Two years later, I directed freshman and sophomore parents and students to the front of the hall on College Night. I spotted Michael, "Good to see you, where is your father?" Pointing in his father's direction, "Dr. Colón, he is in the back." I found my veteran parent, Mr. Jackson, and watched him work his magic. Mr. Jackson nonchalantly walked to the back of the room and invited Mr. Simmons to join him and Mrs. Jackson.

Mr. and Mrs. Jackson had a senior daughter headed to Marquette University. Their son Bryce was a sophomore. It wasn't long before Michael found himself nearly adopted by the Jacksons.

The Jackson family lived near the campus, and Michael often went over after school for a snack before football or soccer practice or hung out after an all-day workday for robotics. One afternoon, Michael inquired about Shelia Jackson and Marquette University. Shelia had built quite a resume highlighting her leadership in community service, student council, and with her youth group. Marquette, along with several other colleges, offered Shelia partial scholarships, Mrs. Jackson explained, which made college more affordable for her family. It was those conversations at the Jackson home that inspired Michael to dream about college.

By the time Michael was a junior, he was the lead engineer on the robotics team and selected as the director of STEM Summit. Michael poured his energy into reading and researching topics like engineering, programming, and building a robot from scratch. Throughout the fall, Michael networked with the adults from The Aerospace Corporation when they were on campus and asked where they went to school, what they majored in, and about work and internships. He learned about Olin College of Engineering, MIT, and RIT, and others closer to home like Cal Poly, SLO, Harvey Mudd, and the prestigious CalTech. One of the top executives of Aerospace took a liking to Michael and offered him a part-time job at the plant the summer before his senior year. His STEM resume was impeccable; he had taken advantage of every opportunity afforded to him in three plus years, and all that was left was to apply to college.

In addition to working at Aerospace on Saturdays, Michael spent most of his summer studying for the SAT. Each morning, Michael woke up at six in the morning to have breakfast with his father before they each went off to work. By 6:30 a.m., Mr.

Simmons put on his vest and with his forefinger, touched his son's heart and whispered, "Guion." This was their code word for dreams. Mr. Simmons had named his son Michael Guion as a tribute to his hero, Guion Bluford, the first African American in space. Mr. Simmons had once dreamed of becoming an aeronautical engineer but left college early to raise Michael on his own.

Michael applied to six engineering programs, and by April he received congratulations from three. In the end, it was ultimately the co-op program at Rochester Institute of Technology that won him over. Mr. Simmons' dream may have been delayed, but that August his son finally took flight and traveled across the country to Rochester, NY, sight unseen. Four years later, "Guion" earned his wings and became the first college graduate in his family.

TRUTH:

If you take nothing else away from this book, consider one question, "Given YOUR resources, what are you doing to optimally utilize them?" As an admission officer, I tended to use this as a good litmus test: *The truth is that no matter what your background, the college application process will require you to have encouragers, realists, gentle pushers, cheerleaders, and mentors.* something I learned from JC Tesone at Vassar College.

What does this look like? I'll give you an academic example. If your high school offers two advanced placement (AP) courses and you take both, then that shows the reader that you have taken the most demanding course load offered. On the other hand, if the top students at your high school are graduating with eight AP courses, and you have taken two, then the list of colleges you have as options is much different than the kid who took the most demanding curriculum made available to him/her.

Do yourself a favor. If your parents attended college, pick their brains, talk to their friends, learn about different careers and fields. Find what interests you, and take their advice. For those of you with siblings in college or recently graduated, inquire about courses they took for different majors, ask what they wish they had done, learned, or read in high school to better prepare them for college. Your siblings and their friends have a wealth of information; utilize them as resources. For some of you, you are like Michael, you have no siblings, or parents who paved the way before you. Ask questions of the adults at your school or parents of friends to learn what is possible, and find people who will help you get there.

The truth is that no matter what your background, the college application process will require you to have encouragers, realists, gentle pushers, cheerleaders, and mentors. Find your village of believers and you will thrive.

> **TIP #4** Take Control. Backwards Engineer Your Academic and Leadership Plan.

TALE:

Shoot For The Moon, But Make A Plan To Get There

"I'm sorry, Mr. Fisher, I know we haven't met, but I don't have Melissa's file. Are you sure she is not assigned to another college counselor?"

"No, I'm sorry, Ms. Colón. Melissa is going to be a sophomore, she hasn't been assigned at all."

Confused, I continued, "I see. Did you still want to come in this summer?"

"Yes, if you have time, we could come in next week." With that, we set a date to meet.

Mr. Fisher had one agenda item: to get his daughter into the best college possible. Ivy League was his preference.

Melissa and Mr. Fisher showed up on time, and he proceeded to do most of the talking. I often turned my attention to the right, where she sat quietly. "Melissa, what is it that you like to do? Want to do? What do you see yourself excelling in over the next three years?" She answered each question in the same tone—not overly enthusiastic, but not disinterested either. As the oldest child, she would be the first to apply to college and traverse the muddy waters of highly selective institutions. Mr. and Mrs. Fisher had both attended college in California, but in the last few years it was no secret the landscape of college admissions had significantly changed.

Melissa talked about enjoying student council. As a freshman, she was involved in a variety of clubs, and at the end of the year, she ran for class council and won. She would lead the sophomores as their class president when school began in just three weeks. "OK, this is good information, Melissa. And where do you dream of attending college?"

Before she could answer, Mr. Fisher chimed in, "We are looking at all the Ivies."

Without acknowledging Mr. Fisher, I kept my focus to my right "Is this true, Melissa? Is that what *you* want?"

Mr. Fisher did not dare interrupt again, and, as if she finally recognized that I was her advocate, Melissa sat up straight and showed me her hazel eyes, "Brown and Columbia are my favorites, but I love UCLA too." With a small grin, she added, "Call me Missy." I smiled back and winked.

Together, the three of us spent the next 50 minutes brainstorming and creating a backwards map. With no guarantees of landing on the moon, we forged ahead. The academic profile of a student is the most important element. Missy would need to be eligible to take four or five advanced placement (AP) courses in her senior year, which meant taking three in junior year that naturally advanced into the next set of APs. I was happy to hear that Melissa had already been assigned to the only AP offered to sophomores, AP European History.

This young lady with the long face, hazel eyes, and straight brown hair was already on her way. She asked questions about the SAT exams, which teachers she might consider getting letters of recommendation from, the necessary grades, and of course her resume. Missy's eyes danced when she spoke of class council, "I think I would like to run for student body president at the end of junior year."

Without hesitation I simply asked, "Just like taking AP Euro is the best move for getting into AP US History, what do you think is the best strategic position to have as a junior to enable you to run for student council president?"

Missy verbalized all of the possibilities and options with an understanding of the political ramifications at an all-girls school; the key was to stay active and visible without hogging all the star leadership roles. Being class president two years in a row would almost guarantee that these savvy girls would vote to give a different student a chance to lead. After 90 minutes of game planning and strategizing, the Fisher family left very happy. In Missy's desire to shoot for the moon, making a plan was the easy part. Working her plan meant hard work, late nights, redrafting term papers, after-school practice, weekend commitments, and the courage to persevere no matter what. *That* was the hard part.

I know you want to know, so I will tell you this, Missy went on to attend Brown University, which is the good news. The GREAT news is this, she followed her plan almost exactly the way we laid it out on that summer day, and most importantly her academic curriculum and grades were nearly perfect. She did run and won the role of student council president. In addition to being a leader on the winning Model United Nations and track teams, Missy also spoke off campus as the lead ambassador of the school. The summer before her final year, she drafted her college essay six times. She was committed to her dreams and climbed every inch of that mountain to get there. In September of her senior year, Missy did not know where she would be twelve months later, but she knew this, she had taken control of this process early on, and she alone was responsible for every decision along the way.

TRUTH:

As a college admission officer, I was always surprised to watch how worked up students were about the college admission process. With time came clarity, and I understand now that this process can make sane people spin out of control solely because s/he believes they have no control. Have no fear. The truth is, you have control over everything that goes into that college application. Yes, I did say everything. Like Missy, with a little planning, you can create a road map as early as the summer before freshman or sophomore year and become armed and ready for that senior year application.

The truth is, you have control over everything that goes into that college application.

Disclosure: not everyone is going to land on the moon. In fact, it takes many stars to align perfectly to receive a "big" envelope from one of the top 20 most selective institutions in the country, but the point here is that it can happen and it does happen. The lessons to glean from Melissa's story are two-fold: plan an academic path that is rigorous and realistic, and build a resume that demonstrates the breadth and depth of your talents and leadership. Remember this, when you shoot for the moon, sometimes you actually get there.

CHAPTER 1:
Resources and Final Note

If you haven't figured it out by now, I like a good plan, a nice laid out example, and some go-to resources! If you didn't read the introduction, go back and read it. I basically explain how I became obsessed with college admissions and I was determined to crack the code. I encourage you to become absorbed in any goal or dream you are trying to attain. Finding a mentor can literally mean finding a human adult to support you, but it can also mean finding something to read, watch, or listen to in order to learn the tools for success. If you'd like to learn more about some of the students mentioned in tale #1, scan the QR code in the resource section at the back of the book and it will take you to the iTunes listing for my podcast, Destination YOUniveristy. There you can hear directly from: Janah (Episode 149-152), Cosette (Episode 121), Caroline (Episode 90), Jalyn (Episode 115), Miles (Episode 100), and Ethan L. (Episode 106).

OK! Now that you've taken action, met your counselor, found the right mentor, and have created a plan, let's dive deep into the number one most important item; academics. In order to have plenty of choices, you will first need a solid academic plan to go along with a major of choice, and a list of colleges that are sure to have the big envelopes coming your way!

CHAPTER 2

YOUR ACADEMIC PLAN

CHAPTER 2:
Introduction

Between the months of November and March, for college admissions officers, there are two seasons, reading season and committee season. During reading season, my job was to simply evaluate what was on the page. The college application, I realized, was the written form of a job interview. Imagine interviewing 25-30 applicants every single day for nearly three months straight. My colored pens wrote notes furiously with each and every application. That was the easy part.

Committee season always proved tough for me. Working in admissions is like being in a constant state of Sophie's Choice. I loved so many students, and most were more than qualified, but at the end of the day, the reality was that we could not admit all of them.

The 5 academic food groups include: English, Math, Science, Social Science, and Modern Language. That was the ideal senior year curriculum.

In committee I would present each applicant. I'd read my notes out loud regarding the number of honors and AP courses, insights from the student's essays, and share any anecdotal remarks from the counselor or teachers. Without fail, the one question that was asked by someone on the committee was this: "What is s/he taking this year?" What the committee member was really asking is, "Does the applicant have all 5 academic food groups in their final year of high school?" The 5 academic food groups include:

English, Math, Science, Social Science, and Modern Language. That was the ideal senior year curriculum. This was typically the last question and after my response, we would take a vote.

Each committee member was allowed to hold up one index card, a red, yellow, or a green card was the way in which our offices voted on the applicants. Majority won the day. During Early Decision committees, a student needed five of nine votes, but during regular decision, an admit needed only two of the three votes to win a green sticker!

This chapter is meant to show you why your academic profile is the most important ingredient in your college application. Ultimately it is your transcript (and test scores if you choose) that will determine where you can apply.

Let's get to it!

DR. C

| TIP #5 | Grades Matter Most. |

TALE:
Just Like A Treadmill, Your Grades Should Have An Incline, Not A Decline.

For eight weeks between September and November, I earned sky miles and hotel points, met hundreds of parents and students, and visited dozens of high schools. This was the marathon that admission officers called "Fall Recruiting Season." While most students were in their senior year, many guests were already previewing colleges as sophomores and juniors. Those were the families who asked questions that piqued my interest and continued to follow me

It is always best to shoot for the A in the honors or advanced placement course. Period.

even more once I became a high school college counselor. After my presentation in the school gym or a hotel ballroom, a line would form with skirt-and-tie wearing young women and men with parents in tow. As one family left, the next introduced themselves, "Hello, Cynthia, nice to meet you. I wanted to ask, is it better to get an A in a regular course or a B in an honors or advanced placement (AP) course?" At first I was stumped by this question, and I am positive I stumbled in my answer the first time. It did not occur to me that this child was asking for permission to enroll in the less challenging course. Never once did I fall for that trap.

The short answer to the stated question is this, it is better to take the more challenging course.

However, there are two things wrong with this question. First, as you plot and plan your academic curriculum every spring, your journey should reflect an increase in rigor. Think of it this way, you do not go to the gym and walk one mile on the treadmill forever, do you? No, you increase the time, the pace, and the incline. And even when it seems like you can barely breathe after 15 minutes, you push yourself to go two more minutes again and again. Before you know it, you have gone from walking one mile to running a 5K. Voila! The same goes for school. Each year you should increasingly challenge your brain and remember that you are training for the marathon you call college. The more you can train in high school, the better prepared you will be for the taxing demands of your college professors. I had to learn the hard way that you cannot write a good 15-page paper overnight.

The second problem inherent in the aforementioned question is that you should not set yourself up for settling for a B. I believe in self-fulfilling prophecy: say it out loud and it becomes your truth. I took a small group communication course in college and, you guessed it, we had to work in small groups. We named our team "Frosted Flakes," and I think you probably can guess how we worked; we were flaky and the professor called us out on it. The moment you tell yourself that the best grade you can achieve is X, then you have already set yourself up to do mediocre work that will satisfy the stated goal. With that said, enter high school with the belief that you can achieve the best grades possible with hard work, dedication, and a commitment to having no regrets.

The real answer is, it is always best to shoot for the A in the honors or advanced placement course. Period.

TRUTH:

More than anything, what you need to understand is this truth: While you will graduate with eight semesters of grades, you will apply to college with six semesters of GPA. What this means is that if you are currently a second semester sophomore, you have already earned 50% of your college GPA. Yes, senior year will matter in terms of which courses you are taking, but whatever grade point average you have on your vision board, you need to reach that goal by the end of junior year. I call this

While you will graduate with eight semesters of grades, you will apply to college with six semesters of GPA.

the 6 versus 8 rule. I have seen more students wish they had a stronger academic record than I can count, and the truth is they have nobody to blame but themselves. So, get to it!

MUST DOS:

1 – Take the harder class when possible.

2 – Live with no regrets. Give 110 percent and you will never wonder what could have been.

48

SHOULD DOS:

1 – Look up colleges you are considering to find the average admitted GPA.

2 – You can do the same for scholarships, looking for the minimum GPA required for eligibility.

The bottom line is this: no matter where you are from, which high school you attend, and what your resources are, your goal should always be for the pace of your grades to be on a steady incline and never a decline. With that said, academic life does not come naturally easy for everyone. Do not beat yourself up over a couple of lower grades in your freshman year. The message here is to get back on that treadmill and keep training. Soon you are physically and mentally stronger, your second wind kicks in, and you discover your optimum performance. You will race to the finish line. I promise, you got this!

TIP #6	Standardized Testing. Take Charge & Tackle The Exam.

TALE:
The SAT Whispers In My Ear

As the Griffin family searched for a summer program for their eldest child, they found a highly regarded program in Baltimore which required the SAT test as an entrance exam. Amie would be the only kid in her middle school to voluntarily take the SAT. When the score arrived, Amie did not understand it, but she thought it was a bit low. Two years passed, and in the fall of her sophomore year, she and her classmates took the PSAT. Amie felt ready to master the exam, but when her score arrived she understood that this was *not* the score she wanted two years henceforth.

As Amie sat in my office she remembered meeting Yvonne while visiting her grandparents, "Ms. Colón, I think Yvonne is known as the 'SAT Whisperer.'" Amie's father had grown up in Pacific Palisades, and, up until recently, the Griffin family spent most Sundays together. The taxing demands of private school, volleyball, soccer, track, and student council made it prohibitive to do almost anything else but homework on the weekends.

A week later, Amie pleaded with her parents to let her work

with the SAT Whisperer. This meant allowing Amie to drive herself to school on Fridays, and after practice, Amie would drive to her grandparents home. With their blessing, Amie got to work. The MIT alumna met Amie the following Sunday to review her SAT and PSAT scores, set goals, and make a timeline. Ambitious in her college dreams, Amie and Yvonne set out an 18-month plan with a goal of increasing her score by 500 points.

Every Friday, Amie was up by six in the morning in order to arrive at school by 7:45 a.m. From 3:15 to 5:00 p.m., Amie practiced passing, shooting, heading, dribbling, and trapping the ball on the soccer field. Even as a sophomore, Amie wanted to improve her game, and for an extra fifteen minutes, she asked her coaches to help her develop strength in her kick and endurance on the field. By 5:30 p.m., Amie was in her car and knew Grandma and Grandpa were waiting with dinner for her and Yvonne. Yvonne carefully designed the first two hours of each meeting to stretch and exercise Amie's brain, complete repetitive math drills, become comfortable with math facts and formulas, and build her knowledge through reading in cross-curricular fields while also developing her analytic skills. The final hour always consisted of a timed practice exam in the area of math, reading, writing and language, or essay writing.

The first two months did not yield an improved score in any section of the exam. Amie was not discouraged. Amie plowed ahead and turned down invitations to meet friends for dinner, a movie, or a party on Friday nights. By February, she and Yvonne began to see movement in her score. Yvonne's lessons grew in difficulty as the skills built on each other from one week to the next. The tipping point came by the end of the sixth month, when

Amie grew her score by 100 points. From Saturday to Thursday, the SAT whispered in her ear, like a hummingbird that wouldn't go away. Every Friday she woke up with determination and a readiness unlike any other day of the week. She was addicted to improving her score, and for the next twelve months she never looked back.

In the spring of her junior year, Amie registered for the SAT. When her score arrived she knew exactly what the numbers represented. That Sunday, Yvonne was invited to the Griffin family dinner. At her seat at the table, Amie left a printed copy of her test scores with one note, "Thank you for 'whispering' in my ear."

One year later, Amie received her acceptance letter to Yale. New Haven, Connecticut, would become her new home. The Griffin family could not be more proud!

TRUTH:

Unfortunately, the SAT or ACT was once a necessary evil part of this process. Since COVID, most colleges have gone Test-Optional or in the case of California, all public institutions are now Test Free. I applaud colleges that have removed standardized tests as a mandatory part of their admission process. Bravo to these colleges for reminding students a one-time exam does not define who they are, nor does it all together predict college success. That said, it is too soon to know if in fact standardized testing will be eliminated forever. If you do not want to take the exam and/ or if you are not inclined to turn in your scores, that is perfectly fine. Two of our Essay Campers (that we know of) did not submit scores. Ashley was admitted to Notre Dame and UCLA and Osose was admitted to Princeton and Brown. I will tell you that many students, especially those applying to top 100 colleges, do take the exam and submit their scores. If you feel that your application will be enhanced by a test score, then I say, "Go for it!"

Here are a few tips I offer my private clients:

1 – Take a practice SAT and ACT exam by junior year.

2 – Based on the results and how comfortable you felt, decide on which exam you will pursue.

3 – Follow Amie's lead and study, get a tutor, or use Khan Academy to improve your score over time.

4 – Use fall and/or spring of junior year to take the exam to simply cross this off your list.

5 – Once you have the scores, it will be up to you if you send them in or not. Remember: YOU have control. Own it!

TIP #7

Visit Colleges As Often
As Possible. The More
The Merrier.

TALE:

*There are plenty of colleges in the sea.
The trick is to start fishing early.*

When I set out to travel the country and sell the story of how Matthew Vassar was a self-made man with no children who set out to create a college equal to Harvard and Yale—but for women, I could name the number of colleges I had visited on one hand, including the two I had attended. I did not understand how important it was to visit colleges until I became a college counselor. As the Director of College Counseling, I traveled every month visiting campuses all over the country. Colleges would group together up to fifty counselors at a time to visit four to six schools. You know why? Colleges know that the best way to sell their institution is to get you to visit. For example, one of my favorite tours was known as COWS, Counselors Observing Wisconsin Schools. We were a full busload of counselors from around the country, and we visited Marquette University, Beloit College, and the University of Wisconsin at Madison. While the story of me eating real ice cream from the real cows on campus is a story for another day, believe me, visiting colleges works. By now I have visited likely two hundred or more colleges, and I can still rattle off some of my favorites: Northwestern, Agnes Scott, DePaul, Spelman, Clark University, Princeton, Indiana University, Miami University (OH), Denver University, St. Louis University, Duke, Redlands, UNLV, UCSB, and of course, USC.

What has been most interesting to me are the reasons I fall in love with these institutions of higher learning. They are not the same each time. For some, I love the beauty of the campus, others I love the people I meet, another favorite has the most number of statues in the US—one has a pineapple on top of the roof—and sometimes it is simply the traditions that come with a school that is over 150 years old. You never know what is going to tug at your heartstrings, so get out there and explore, find your potential suitors.

TRUTH:

I'm going to say what parents do not usually want to hear: choosing a college is a gut instinct. Like choosing a boyfriend or girlfriend, you know when you know. Unfortunately, like love, there is not always a mutual attraction. But, with any luck, by the time you are a senior, you will have found a handful of colleges that can make you happy.

There is no replacement for actually visiting a college campus. To see the buildings and landscape, to hear the marching band practicing on the field, to speak with real students

When you visit a place that you know is not right for you, do not fret. Rather, take comfort in knowing that you are one step closer in finding the one that is.

on campus, and to smell and taste the cuisine while visiting the student center is the best way to meet your prospective match. While it may not be possible to traverse the Great Plains, Rocky Mountains, New England, coastal cities, or the southern belle states, do what you can and you will be the better for it. Some of the best tours were ones I randomly took on my way to a farther destination, like University of Pittsburgh, University of Nebraska, and Oregon State. Even if you cannot take an official tour, if you can get out of the car and walk around for thirty minutes, you can capture the feel of a campus.

Sometimes your gut tells you right away whether this is a school for you or not. But sometimes it takes a few visits to different types of colleges to begin to find the right fit. When you visit a place that you know is not right for you, do not fret. Rather, take comfort in knowing that you are one step closer in finding the one that is.

HERE ARE MY RECOMMENDATIONS:
If you are visiting college booths at a College Fair (LIVE or on Zoom) do the following:

1 – You must dress for success. When you look good, you feel good, and when you feel good, you smile. So go wash your face, put on your best shirt, and introduce yourself.

2 – Anchor yourself with good questions. You only need a few good open-ended questions instead. For example, "Tell me about the available

When you look good, you feel good, and when you feel good, you smile. So go wash your face, put on your best shirt, and introduce yourself.

majors for someone with an interest in science or writing" versus "Do you have a journalism major?" Or, "Please share what students love most about campus life" versus "Do you have fraternities and sororities?" Do you see the difference? Avoid the "Yes/No" questions.

3 – Familiarize yourself with the difference between private and public, liberal arts colleges versus universities, and single gender colleges. Understand there are two-year colleges, four-year colleges, technical, culinary, and specialized colleges. I encourage you to use the "Goldilocks" method and try them all on for size!

ONCE YOU ARE READY FOR LIVE ON CAMPUS TOURS FOLLOW THIS PROTOCOL:

Before Your Arrival:

1 – Plan Ahead. Go online to the college website, click on ADMISSIONS, and find the place where you can reserve a spot for an undergraduate admissions tour.

2 – What is a campus tour? The campus tour is typically led by a student ambassador and can last anywhere from 60 to 90 minutes.

3 – Do I also need to attend an information session? An admission officer typically leads an information session and likely reads applications and has a role in making a decision on prospective applicants. If you have time for both a tour and session, do both. If not, choose one and reserve a spot.

Once on Campus:

1 – Arrive early to find parking.

2 – Come prepared with a few questions. See above.

3 – Turn off your phone and keep your eyes open. You will be

amazed at what you learn by reading what is posted on bulletin boards, picking up the school newspaper, and watching and listening to students.

4 – Take a few photos. Use the photos to capture something that strikes you and/or will help jog your memory later.

5 – Ask a staff member for the name and email address of the admission officer assigned to your school. If you want to follow up with an email (or handwritten note) it is good to know to whom to address it.

Immediately After Your Visit:

Grab your phone or a college journal and take notes. Spend five minutes free writing. Do not overthink this, you need to write your gut reactions: the good, the bad, and the ugly. Jot down bullet notes, write a paragraph or draw or doodle, or sketch whatever comes to mind. Be sure to journal something within a couple of hours after leaving.

> **TIP #8**
>
> Show Up On TIME.
> Keep TRACK Of Your
> Accomplishments. Say
> THANK YOU.

TALE:
High School: Your Job Interview For College

Several colleges out there have an added space for applicants to answer some obscure question that is only for that particular college. At Vassar ours was called "My Space." It was literally a blank sheet of paper where you could do, write, draw, paint, and submit just about anything. Some of the ones worth keeping include a single shoe delivered with the message, "Now I've got one foot in the door." Another student created a self-portrait of himself made entirely of jelly beans, and one of my personal favorites was a children's book authored and illustrated by the applicant.

As fun as it was to discover each student's "My Space," when asked about that portion of the application, I instead turned my focus to what I believe are the three key habits to ensuring that three important parts of your application (transcript, resume, and letters of recommendation) are as stellar as possible. Let me put it this way, while in high school, you are on a three- or three-and-a-half-year interview. Spending hours, days, or weeks on that one obscure question or constructing a scale model of the walkway over the Hudson is not going to earn you the big envelope alone. The transcript, resume, and letters of recommendations are items that will evolve over time and cannot be ideally created or invented at the last minute. Here are the three key habits to develop based on my experience as a college admission officer and college counselor.

Show up on TIME:

Nayeli, "Naya," lived thirty-five miles from school, which can be hours on the freeway in Southern California. She and her father, Mr. Nuñez, left the house at 6 a.m. every morning. While not completely practical to live so far away from school, the Nuñez family lived in Long Beach for its accessibility to the metro, walkable neighborhoods, trendy restaurants, and nearby ocean. A huge proponent of utilizing mass transportation, Naya's father had taught her how to navigate the city via trains and buses. On the rare occasion that Mr. Nuñez had a meeting near home, Naya was able to get to school on her own and was never late to class. Naya loved school, loved her teachers, and used her time after school to get involved in everything while waiting for Dad to pick her up and take the two-hour drive home. Naya spent time in teachers' classrooms practicing her Model United Nations competition speeches, writing for the literary magazine, and building robots with her friends in the science lab. Naya was a favorite among her teachers, but not just because she was likable, it was the respect she showed for education.

While some peers who lived twenty minutes from school showed up ten minutes late to class, latte in hand, Naya would never think to walk in and interrupt a teacher's classroom. More than this, Nayeli knew that missing a quiz or part of a test would result in coming to class at lunch or after school, and she had far too many friends and activities to catch up with. For Naya, it simply was not worth the trouble of being late, so she vowed to always be on time.

Keep TRACK of Accomplishments:

Raised by a single mom, Ignacio "Nacho" Gonzales thrived since he could walk. Nacho sang, danced, played the piano and electric keyboard, but that is what he did for fun. In an attempt to find Nacho's talents, mom enrolled him in all the typical and atypical sports and hobbies. Ms. Gonzales found her son enjoying sushi by the age of three, excelling in karate at a rapid speed, and drawn to the vibrant colors of anime. His dedication to the art of karate had earned him a junior black belt by the time he was fourteen years old. It was no surprise that Nacho worked as an assistant to his Sensei while continuing to hone his craft and earn his black belt in high school. As a junior, he led the art club, won local and regional awards for his anime drawings, and had shone his work all over Southern California.

Though difficult to keep track of all of Nacho's achievements, his mother recorded everything, just as she had when he was a child. The large plastic purple file box held every award Nacho had received since earning his white belt. Every June and December, without fail, Nacho sat with his mother and recorded his honors. The printed document affixed to the refrigerator served as fuel to push forward, do more, and get better.

Say THANK You:

Niko grew up in a large home: two parents, and three siblings, each with their own room. Niko's parents lived a very different life as children, having grown up in the Midwestern town of

Kokomo, Indiana. With grandparents as farm owners and union workers, Niko's parents went out of their way to inspire the notion of imagination and reading instead of the perfunctory teenage pastimes, such as, television, video and computer games, or movie watching. Niko much preferred setting up obstacle courses in the backyard, tinkering with cars, or inventing science experiments. As a result, Niko was addicted to "how-to" videos found on the Internet and developed an unquenchable thirst for knowledge. He came prepared for class each day and peppered his teachers with questions that often began with "why." While some teachers might become frustrated with the constant inquisition, Niko's genuine interest showed through, and that is what made it special. Niko's questions spurred new conversations and discussions in the classroom, often taking the topic to a deeper level. Teachers loved it.

As he exited the classroom, a simple, "Thanks, Mr. Cendejas," or "Great lecture Dr. Edwards," melted off his lips, and his eyes beamed with excitement.

TRUTH:

Believe it or not, the counselor and teachers are very honest in those letters of recommendation, and before you know it you will need to ask them to become your advocate for college. As effusive as they are with lauding your accomplishments in the classroom and leadership in the community, a teacher has the ability to paint the picture of who you are as a person in a few words. Hear me when I tell you that they want nothing more than for

A teacher has the ability to paint the picture of who you are as a person in a few words.

you to succeed. By showing up on time and keeping track of your accolades, you will have plenty of material to give your teacher to write about—this is half the battle. It is the appreciation you offer at the end of class and the genuine interest you show in class that will speak volumes.

I used to give teachers a tip of ending a letter in one of a few ways: "Calyn is the best student in period 5," or "Larry is the best student I have taught this year," or "Montana is one of the best writers I have seen in the last five years," or "Brandon is by far one of my best students in my twenty year career." Using this one sentence at the beginning or end of a letter, a teacher has clearly given us the information we need. And there are several adjectives that you can use here: best leader, kindest student, most compassionate, best debater, the hardest working, etc.

The truth is, you have a clear strength as a student and as a contributor to your community. Whatever it is, be the best at it. With each day in high school, you have an opportunity to design and create who you are to the world. If you have a habit of being late, no problem; commit to being on time for the next thirty days, and it will become a habit.

If you are a sophomore and have yet to get involved on campus, no worries; there are plenty of organizations that have

With each day in high school, you have an opportunity to design and create who you are to the world.

been waiting for you to join, so get moving. And if you have never thought about thanking your teachers, it is the best gift you can give to any and all of them. A simple, "Thank you," on your way out the door will go a long way. Trust me, s/he will notice.

CHAPTER 2:
Resources and Final Note

If you'd like to learn more about some of the students mentioned in tale #6, scan the QR code in the resource section at the back of the book and it will take you to the iTunes listing for my podcast, Destination YOUniveristy. There you can hear directly from: Ashley (Episode 112), Osose (Episode 110). If you want to become a "Dreamer" you can learn more about Dream College Academy (DCA) on my website, www.drcynthiacolon. com.

Well now, look at you already at the end of Chapter 2! Bravo. Your grades and test scores will determine which set of colleges you are eligible for and the earlier you begin your college search, the better prepared you will become! Oh, and don't forget: be on time, keep track of activities and say thank you. These key habits will get you off to a great start in controlling your own destiny in the college admission process. Remember, 90 percent of your application happens well before senior year. Don't put off tomorrow what you can do today. You control this process.

Next step: fill your resume.

Let's get to it!

CHAPTER 3

YOUR RESUME PLAN

CHAPTER 3:
Introduction

There are nearly 3,000 four-year colleges across the country. And if I'm being honest, the average acceptance rate is 65%. If you are reading this book, I promise you *will* be admitted to several colleges. And while my experience as an Admission Officer and Director of College Counseling had me working with students who were interested in some of the most competitive colleges, this book is meant for every college bound teen. When I was your age I did just enough school work to stay competitive among

In any applicant pool, the Academic Qualities (AQs) will be similar among the students, but it is Personal Qualities (PQs) that will help you stand out.

my peers, but believe me, I was not pulling all-nighters for that extra + in my A. I took several Honors courses and not a single AP course. Yep. It's true.

What I fell in love with in high school was all the fun stuff. I was a cheerleader, in Key Club, on the drill team, and was the student body president in my senior year. I loved planning the student assemblies and giving the daily announcements over the school intercom. Like some of you, I simply loved being involved.

Whether your interests lie in clubs, service, athletics, performing arts, student council, or competitive organizations, the message in this chapter is to get involved and do something. Don't get tied to the traditional examples offered in this chapter. There are a million ways to do something you actually enjoy. I can recall some of my essay campers who wrote about spearfishing, map collections, sushi making, beat making, thrift shopping, crocheting, reading, numerous shoe collections, and simply taking care of siblings or ailing parents or grandparents. All of this counts and belongs on your resume. I promise you.

While your Academic Qualities (AQs) will get your foot in the door, it is your personal resume that will ultimately get you admitted. In any applicant pool, the AQs will be similar among the students, but it is Personal Qualities (PQs) that will help you stand out. And while you do not have to fill up your "dance card" with a litany of clubs, this chapter is a reminder that interested students make for interesting applicants.

Let's get to it!

TIP #9 Do Something You Enjoy.

TALE:
Something To Talk About

Once in a while, an applicant comes across as seemingly "perfect." There is Brenda who wants to become a nurse, has spent the last two years volunteering at the local hospital, earns extra spending money by babysitting, and completed her Gold Award for Girl Scouts by making and collecting warm blankets for newborn babies. Or Noah who has played soccer since he was three years old, is now the captain of his school and club team, has collected cleats and uniforms each year to deliver to young players in Mexico, leads the Future Business Leaders of America club, and wants to major in business with an emphasis in sports management. WOW. Impressive.

If you are in middle school or a freshman in high school, this should not sound familiar. These "perfect" (no such thing) applicants did not happen overnight. Every student goes through a process of figuring out the answer to the following questions: Who? What? When? How? and Why? (WWWHW). Who do you want to spend time with? What do you enjoy? When do you have time in your day? How can you contribute your talents? Why is this important to you?

Just like your grades and test scores tell the story of what admission officers often call your "AQs," Academic Qualities, your co-curricular resume will describe for the reader your "PQs," Personal Qualities. At the risk of making it sound as though your academic profile is less important, I want to remind you that every single applicant comes to the table with a grade point average and a test score. For now, let's assume everyone begins on equal footing with regards to AQs.

As your college counselor, I suggest you begin developing your resume sooner rather than later. For some students, their entire resume is filled with performing arts: plays, dance, and acting competitions. A similar student might enjoy performing arts as well but only participates in the fall because her primary contribution is on the robotics team, which competes in the spring. For students who most enjoy spending their time on the field or on the court, they might contribute their hidden talent by singing in the church choir. Emerging leaders may discover a passion for speaking and hone that craft by joining the Speech and Debate Team or by becoming a school ambassador. There is no perfect pathway to college. There is also nobody else like you. You are unique, and the possibilities are endless on what to do and how to immerse yourself in the joy of school.

If joining new clubs and meeting new friends is hard for you, rest assured you are not alone. Why not invite a classmate to join you at the club lunch meeting? Or better yet, ask Mom or Dad to bake or buy some cookies to bring to the meeting, and you are sure to be a hit with others. The longer you wait to join a club, try out for a team, and explore new activities, the easier it will

BE COMMITTED. GET ADMITTED.

become to stay glued to your smart phone and video games. That may suit you now, but once you are applying to college, you will have nothing to talk about and risk the chance of having the AQs, but all too few PQs.

Your only job in life right now is to go to school. So why not make it fun, try new adventures, hone a skill, and get out of your comfort zone? Adults today believe that there are way too many students attached to their phones, computers, and video games; and as a result their heads are staring at a screen instead of looking up and out into the world around them. Push yourself to embrace high school, because one day you will wish you were a kid again.

Get out there and give us all something to talk about!

TRUTH:

Reading an application was exciting to me; it was like taking a tour of the student's life and dissecting who he is or what she is most proud of. On a typical day of reading, I captured the most impressive activities and adventures of the applicant. I noted the personal essay topics *When you become interested in life around you, you become a more interesting applicant* and the personality that came through. I highlighted how the counselor and teachers described a student's contributions in and out of the classroom.

On occasion, I would breeze through an application much more quickly than others. I closed the red file and thought, "Did I miss something?" Invariably, the answer was no. Unfortunately, there was not much to talk about in the file.

What you do outside the classroom says just as much as, if not more than, what you do in the classroom. Go on, get up and discover the answers to Who? What? When? How? and Why? When you become interested in life around you, you become a more interesting applicant *and* have plenty to talk about!

Here are a few recommendations for building your resume:

Freshmen: Explore: Take time to meet new people, and try a number of activities, clubs, arts, and sports. ADVICE: Join, run, lead, spike, pitch, defend, act, paint, or dance; just don't let this year pass without doing something.

Sophomores: Experience: Think outside of the box and outside of your traditional school clubs and organizations. Maybe get a job, try a club sport, support a local non-profit, or contribute to your church or synagogue. Try one thing that is out of your comfort zone, you might surprise yourself!

Juniors: Elevate: What does this mean? Don't wait to become a leader, go out and break personal records and/or sing your heart out on stage. Become the applicant I know you can be!

Seniors: Enjoy! You have approximately 300 days left with your classmates, be sure to spend quality time with friends. Have faith that your future is bright. Create lasting memories with every adventure, competition, performance, game, leadership and service opportunity.

TIP #10

Three Ways To Do
Community Service.

TALE:

How We Serve-ice Our Communities

The very act of doing something with no expectation of getting something in return can fill your soul. Your act may be as simple as helping during a Thanksgiving food drive, donating your artistic skills to design the poster for the school musical, or giving up buying a daily beverage for a week to make a financial donation towards the senior class gift. What most high school students fail to grasp is that there is no "right" way to do service. When it comes to considering how you might serve your community, bear in mind that you have three options. You can give your time, your talent, or your treasure, each of them is equally important.

While recruiting for Vassar College, I was often asked about community service. Over time, I came up with three examples to share as my answer. Consider the following three students as examples of serving on a local, regional, or national level.

TIME: *Kendra grew up in a suburb of Los Angeles. Beginning at the age of 5, her summer was spent at Ballona Beach Cities Day Camp. Shy and nervous at first, with each year that passed, Kendra became more courageous in moving from swimming to paddleboarding, surfing,* *and kayaking. New campers began to look to Kendra for encouragement and an enthusiastic "You can do it" on the sands of the Pacific Ocean. It was no surprise that Kendra was invited to become a junior counselor, lead songs after the aquatics activities, and help with the "New Bees" at camp. Kendra returned every year selflessly. She did not know what a profound difference she made, and yet she gave up her summer to ensure that campers like Becky, Paul, Gemma, Jules, and Malik had an enjoyable time at the best beach camp in town.*

TALENT: *Roy was always a mover and a shaker from Seattle, Washington. I never understood how Roy could get students to give up a Saturday to clean National Parks, build houses, or tutor middle school students, but he did. He delivered a message that tugged at your heartstrings, and before you knew it, you were sucked in. Roy's mother was a phlebotomist, and so each year he led the Red Cross Blood Drive. There were plenty of students and teachers who qualified as potential donors. One by one, Roy made the rounds at lunch, "What would you do if you could save three lives in just 20 minutes?" Intrigued by the question that never failed to engage others, Roy would spend the next seven minutes convincing everyone at that lunch table to sign up to give blood. But signing up did not always translate to showing up. Three days before the blood drive, he sent a mass email reminder. The evening before, Roy sent individual text messages. And the morning of your donation, a mass blind text was sent as a reminder and thank you. Each year the number of donors increased, and the Red Cross recognized him for his efforts.*

TREASURE: *In November of Kelby's freshman year, she and her family volunteered at "Feed my Sheep" on Thanksgiving morning. Kelby was inspired by the diversity of people who came together to serve and be served. People of all races, age, religious and socio–economic* *backgrounds from all over Delaware County were in one place to celebrate life and give thanks. Over the course of the next few weeks, she overheard her parents talking with community leaders who said they wanted to expand the operation to serve the number of people in need. Just before winter break, Kelby headed to her art class to finally collect her items that were recently fired in the kiln. She had made a set of four bowls for her family—each slightly larger in size—for her sister, herself, mom, and dad. Walking home that day, a light bulb went off. "Shepherding through Soup" was born. Every fall, all of the bowls produced by Muncie Central High School students go on sale and serve as an entrance ticket for the bottomless soup event held in the school cafeteria. After her first year, Kelby partnered with cross-town rival, Delta High School, and increased the funds raised by 125 percent.*

When you think back on a time when you have given your time, talents, or treasure to a worthy cause, you cannot help but smile. Your daily, weekly, or annual deposit, no matter how small or large, will impact others, and that is how you serve-ice your community.

TRUTH:

There are hundreds of ways in which we can serve our local, regional, national, and/or global community. When you discover your gifts, embrace them, and then utilize them to change our world in whatever capacity you can. There is no right way to serve, only your way.

The truth is this: giving back is one of the greatest life lessons we can learn when we are young. I want to encourage you to find a way to give your time, talent, or treasure. If literally serving soup or reading books to youngsters is not your calling, I promise you, this is perfectly fine. College campuses everywhere need leaders, coordinators, motivators, movers and shakers, as well as, altruistic do-gooders. Stay true to who you are and serve-ice your community!

College campuses everywhere need leaders, coordinators, motivators, movers and shakers, as well as, altruistic do-gooders. Stay true to who you are and serve-ice your community!

| TIP #11 | Lessons Of An Athlete Go Beyond The Court. |

TALE:
Habits of a Team

A student of the game, Coach Mitch had turned down an athletic scholarship to play at a small college to instead become the team manager for the successful University of Kansas, a Division I college team in the Midwest. Bringing his knowledge to the Viking team that year, Coach Mitch and the team hobbled through the end of the season with mixed success. By the end of the year, some families chose to transfer in search of a school with a winning program. Coach Mitch wished them well, "Dr. Colón and I will always welcome you back home."

His plan was simple: get the boys on a solid and consistent training and eating plan, methodically practice and master the basic skills of basketball, and play against the best competition possible, as often as possible. Each day practice was a grind: footwork, dribbling, passing, shooting, and rebounds. A few more students gave up, but most stuck with the program as they gradually noticed personal improvement. With early success in pre-season, the team made a commitment to Coach Mitch and did exactly what he said. They won and won often. This was great, except it was time to reorganize the teams in our league, and our recent success meant our competitor schools voted our team to move up to the next league. This would not be good for winning. When I delivered the news to Coach Mitch, I was startled by his reaction, "That is the best news I've heard all year. Great!"

In his second full year as head coach, Mitch led with enthusiasm at every workout, practice, and every game. His quest to win was nothing short of preparing for a David versus Goliath battle. This was like being the best AAA baseball team and then moving up to play against all the top major league teams the following year. We had 1,000-1 odds, but Coach Mitch understood that playing against the best only made his team hungrier. Coach repeated his philosophy of consistency of actions leading to excellent habits. The team had tasted success in the summer and now bought into the idea that winning was a short-term goal, but consistent improvement would prevail. He believed in his boys and so they followed.

That season, the Varsity Viking Basketball team went from failure to failure with absolute enthusiasm. They lost every single game with the exception of one near the end of the season. At the end of the season, Coach explained that the strength of our league teed us up to receive a berth in postseason play. Moved to compete against a more appropriate group of schools, play-off games began. Two weeks later, we won the coin toss for the location of the semi-final game against the number 1 seed. The gym was packed, and the game came down to the final seconds, and we landed victorious. With one game left, the California Interscholastic Federation (CIF) Championship title was within our grasp.

The reigning champs were not prepared for our team. Our

Vikings stayed on them for thirty-two minutes, a habit not formed overnight but over time. Their hard and fast play was evident, only achieved by practicing the habit of quick thinking, watching everywhere, and relying on teammates to be there. The Vikings' ball skills had been honed by repetition of shooting the ball correctly every single day. And their fierce commitment to rebounds only proved their commitment to win. At the end of the thirty-two minutes, the unlikely winner proved to everyone that natural talent can only take you so far, but when honed, with repetition and commitment, talent can be transformed into the habit of excellence. It is the habit of excellence that wins championships. Bravo, Vikings!

TRUTH:

There are a multitude of lessons woven in this tale: quitting is not an option, transferring is not the answer, failure is a good thing, and, with consistency, excellent habits are formed. If you can join a team sport in high school, do it. Even if you are not the best player on the team, even if you sit on the bench more than you play, do it. The life lessons of failure, team, success, and hard work are served up best in a team sport.

The life lessons of failure, team, success, and hard work are served up best in a team sport.

Over the last decade or two, there has been a movement of more and more high school aged students joining club team sports. Whether it is travel ball for baseball or softball, club volleyball, or private weekend tournaments for basketball, thousands of high school athletes have decided to try and master one sport in lieu of attempting several. This has altered the landscape of high school athletics. The would-be football, basketball, and baseball player now only participates in winter basketball. The would-be volleyball, soccer, and softball player now only participates with her club volleyball team year-round in hopes of receiving a college scholarship. While this is a family decision, and you will choose what is best for your son or daughter, please hear me out:

1 – When students are engaged with their peers, teachers, and coaches, they feel more connected and happier at school.

2 – Even if you choose to participate outside of school, give your talents to your own high school as well.

3 – Receiving a full or partial athletic scholarship is tough, be sure to never take your eyes off the real prize: academics.

4 – Whatever you choose, whether you are winning or failing, be sure you never lose your joy and enthusiasm!

TIP #12 — Theater Crew Can Lead To Multiple Majors.

TALE:
Do What You Love And The Major Will Follow.

Josiah was the quintessential "Mr. Everything." Being good at nearly everything wasn't always that easy. Never quite big enough or fast enough for football, instead he tried out for the tennis team. He sang well enough, but was much better on stage, memorizing lines and delivering them with heart. Though well-known throughout many different cliques on campus, Josiah purposely chose the safer route and was elected by his classmates for Class Council instead of running for Student Council. By the time he was a senior, Josiah was Senior Class Vice-President, captain of the tennis team, actor, robotics and Key Club leader, and Josiah even led the church youth group on weekends.

With a father who worked night shifts and a mother who was often missing in action, Josiah actively avoided his home as much as possible and found love at school. The early part of the fall brought the opportunity to take his frustrations out on those yellow-green tennis balls, swinging back and forth across the net. Early October was filled with rehearsals, cast gatherings, and an excuse to help with the stage sets on weekends. Josiah found his people in theater more than any other organization. He found friends who were odd yet quirky, smart yet awkward, joyful yet sad, strong yet weak, and each was driven, ambitious, and hard-working in the face of some adversity in his or her life.

Robotics, Key Club, and Class Council kept Josiah busy throughout the year, and especially in the spring, but it was the theater that kept him physically on campus. Even when meetings and robot sessions ended at 8 p.m., Josiah could always find Mrs. Kofenya working with actors or Mr. Hartigan using power tools with the student crew. Like a father teaches his son how to change a tire or swing a bat, so too would Mr. Hartigan teach Josiah a new skill with the jigsaw power tool. Josiah was grateful and took those new talents with him to the robotics build team. When the robotics team competed in the annual FIRST competition in the spring of his junior year, Josiah invited Mr. Hartigan to come watch and support the team. Mr. Hartigan obliged and happily wore his safety glasses to be on the floor with the team. Josiah beamed as his mentor assisted with twisting and tweaking of a few pieces on the team robot.

TRUTH:

Josiah added to his resume year after year by spending as many as 10-15 hours per day on campus. He literally filled his "dance card" with nearly every club, organization, and performing arts event. What he did in four years became an elongated resume. Good for him. What I love about Josiah's resume is that as diverse as his involvement seems, as an admission officer, I could put it into two categories: service (serving his school, his church, and the community) and "hands on" building skills (theater crew and the robotics team). There are a number of majors that Josiah could list and it would make complete sense to the reader. He could do theater, production, engineering, public policy, or anything along those lines.

When you submit your application, your ultimate goal is to easily connect the dots for your reader in a compelling way. In other words, when you declare that you want to be an engineer, doctor, lawyer, entrepreneur, or teacher, the reader has to believe you. Your resume helps to build your case with evidence. If Josiah declared mechanical engineering or wanted to major in film or theater as a set producer, I would be sold because his resume helps clearly and easily paint the picture that he is who he says he is. Capiche?

When you submit your application, your ultimate goal is to easily connect the dots for your reader in a compelling way.

CHAPTER 3:
Resources and Final Note

This chapter got me thinking about so many Dreamers and Campers that have excellent examples of involvement. To hear about what they did to stand out, scan the QR code in the resource section at the back of the book and it will take you to the iTunes listing for my podcast, Destination YOUniveristy. There you can hear directly from: Bonnie (Episode 98), Hunter (Episode 112), Lauren (Episode 136), Ivy (Episode 135), Jeffrey (Episode 129), Kenzie (Episode 132), John (Episode 128), and Julio (Episode 134). And if you want to become a "Dreamer" you can learn more about Dream College Academy (DCA) on my website, www.drcynthiacolon.com. It is in module three where we discuss your PQs, involvement, and leadership.

In your four years of high school you want to Explore, Experience, Elevate, and Enjoy! In that order! As you develop your resume, take a pause once in a while and reflect on the themes and connections that have filled your dance card. Why did you choose that cause, sport, organization or leadership role? Is there a tie with the major you

At the end of the day, what you do will become your resume, why you do it will become your essay

have in mind? At the end of the day, what you do will become your resume, why you do it will become your essay (more on this in chapter 6). WHY you do anything matters to college admission officers because it matters to you. Interested students make for interesting applicants. The next chapter will offer examples of students who have developed a compelling "why," be it on accident or on purpose.

Now, let's get to it!

CHAPTER 4

YOUR LEADERSHIP PLAN

CHAPTER 4:
Introduction

If you are a natural leader and/or planning to apply to top 100 colleges, this chapter is for you. Colleges are in search of all types of leaders, and top colleges look for those who leave an impact. While reviewing applicants, I had a form to jot down notes of things that stood out for each candidate. At the top of this form a blank space was reserved ONLY for applicants who held key leadership positions, such

Colleges are in search of all types of leaders, and top colleges look for those who leave an impact.

as Student Body President, Editor in Chief of the Yearbook or Newspaper, Captain of a major sport on campus, Girl Scout Gold Award Recipient or Eagle Scout. This spot was also reserved for the even more rare awards like a regional or national champion, which could range from sports, research, science fairs, or visual or performing arts competitions.

I called this blank space "The Line for Five." Believe it or not, sometimes I went a couple of days before filling in that Line for Five. For as competitive as it is to gain admission to Vassar College, you have to remember, just like there is only one valedictorian per school, the same is true for the campus leaders. And lest you think that the Gold Award or Eagle Scout is not a big deal, less than 6% of all Girl and Boy Scouts are eligible and earn these awards. And Hello, I mean if you are a state or national champion, I mean really. Mic drop, please.

Having worked with thousands of students, I can tell you this:

even if you are not one of these "Line for Five" students, each and everyone of you can develop what I call your "Coolness Factor" and/or a "Coolness Project." In tale #13, Wayne creates a coolness factor by just being himself and following his heart and love for his school. In tale #14, Cathy finds herself in a situation that she cannot ignore, which becomes a passion project that leaves a legacy. Olivia's story in tale #15 offers a perfect example of how combining something you love to do (help kids) with something you have to do (build a resume that shows evidence of your proposed major) can readily create your coolness project.

Now, let's get to it!

TIP #13 | Leadership Doesn't Always Come In A Title.

TALE:
When The Going Gets Tough, The Tough Don't Get Going!

Staring out the library window, there were only eight players on the football field. With the resignation of the head football coach, the parents of our young men began entertaining the opportunity of completing their high school years at another school. Lured away by the promise of playing time and a chance at being recruited to play college ball, students' and families' loyalty faded. As Wayne watched his buddies and teammates leave his alma mater, Wayne remained resolute. His decision to remain at St. Bernard made him the sole senior to return as a varsity football member. As I sat there staring out the window, I was sure the news had been delivered to Wayne that Dr. Colón had canceled varsity football for that season.

With only eight players, it was not clear that St. Bernard would even field a junior varsity team. Wayne called his loyal brothers and walked around at freshmen orientation recruiting others to join the JV squad. By the end of the first day of school, there were 29 students at the football meeting, including six seniors. Practice began the next day.

As a new principal, I did not realize our league by-laws stated that seniors were not allowed to play on the junior varsity team. I made my plea in writing and requested the team be allowed to play no more than two seniors at a time. The league voted against our request. The conversation lasted no more than four minutes, including the time it took to vote. I was angry. Six seniors made a stance that academics and loyalty to school trumped a fleeting promise on the field. As educators, this is what we teach our students: to stand for something bigger than themselves. I was worried Wayne and his teammates would find their efforts futile.

By 3:30 p.m., the six seniors, head coach, and assistant coach gathered in the conference room. Like pulling off a band-aid, the sting was hot and quick. The tears rolled down their young faces, but when I looked at Wayne, I began to shed my own. Ever positive, Coach said, "We're going to need your leadership on the sidelines. We still need you. You're a Viking." Without hesitation, Wayne was the first to say, "You got it, Coach! I'm in."

All six seniors remained on the team. They rode on the bus, wore their jerseys on the sidelines, carried water to underclassmen, fetched balls, and even called out plays. The October home game became Senior Night and the 7 p.m. start made for the perfect setting for Wayne and his five comrades to shine in the Friday night lights. The Vikings were 6-0, and on this night, they faced their toughest competitor. The mini army of six seniors wore their home team jerseys, khaki bottoms, and matching blue and gold tennis shoes. Wayne led by encouraging players on the sidelines, delegating assistance for more water, more tape, etc. The game lived up to the hype and proved nerve-wracking for a full four quarters.

I grinned from ear to ear as I watched Wayne give a heated talk to receiver "Lil Tone." Like a drill sergeant, Wayne got in his face and yelled, "Lil Tone, you're losing your fire!" Down by a field goal with less than two minutes to play... A second down, eight yards to go, resulted in a gain of two yards. Eleven boys huddled, and the crowd stood on their feet. The quarterback scrambled, the ball hung in the air, and fell directly into the hands of Lil Tone who ran like the wind. Touchdown! We were now 7-0.

Two weeks later, the Vikings went undefeated and became League Champions. Wayne and his teammates proved once and for all, when the going gets tough, it is indeed the tough that stay, fight, and win!

TRUTH:

One does not become a leader simply because of a title. No. The label is often given once you have proven you are a leader. Your peers are more likely to vote for you on Class Council or Student Council because you have humbly served without a title in prior years. You will earn your spot as editor in chief, captain, lead delegate or actor once you have proven your skills and commitment to the said organization.

When Wayne decided to remain a Viking, he was not the captain of the team. Wayne was a student who wanted to have a great senior year. Doesn't every teen want that? Wayne's "why" was simple: do the right thing for team,

One does not become a leader simply because of a title. No. The label is often given once you have proven you are a leader.

school, and family. It was Wayne's personal will and loyalty to school that "accidentally" made him a leader for others to look up to. THIS became Wayne's "Coolness Factor." His hometown hero story made the local newspaper and he won the Student Of The Year Award, an honor given to him by 4 Star General, Kevin P. Chilton.

If you should find yourself in a situation of whether or not to do the right thing, I can guarantee choosing to do the right thing will lead you down a more prosperous path.

| TIP #14 | Stand Up For What You Believe And Leave A Legacy. |

TALE:
Take A Stand, Take Action, And Take On The World

Regina walked into the office teary eyed, and her best friend, Karla, was there to explain. On the round lunch table, Regina and Karla saw the "N" word boldly written across Regina's notebook. Regina told Ms. Reynolds she felt bad because she made the freshman volleyball team and so many others had not. Distraught, Ms. Reynolds tried to console her, "You are kind, Regina, but that is no reason for anyone to use that word. I will need to let Ms. Colón know what happened."

By the end of the day, nearly everyone on the girls JV and varsity volleyball team knew of the incident and were appalled that a freshman had the audacity to use that word. The school community had survived an "N" word incident just six months prior in the spring semester. Just when wounds were healing, the students of color would feel demoralized yet again.

Cathy Oh, President of the newly founded Diversity Club, spent most of her time at lunch listening to students. The minority students felt unwelcomed and uncomfortable on campus, while the Caucasian students tiptoed around their peers, not knowing what to say or what not to say. A deep chasm was growing by the day and there was palpable tension in the air.

One afternoon, Cathy came to me with an idea. She suggested a sort of documentary, interviewing a cross section of students from all grade levels and all backgrounds. At the next Diversity Club meeting, Cathy gave the members a sheet of paper with10 questions to answer. The key for Cathy was to not make this movie about race, but to be inclusive of the "Big 8": race, religion, socio-economic status, ability/disability, ethnicity, age, gender, and sexual orientation. The top five questions that elicited the most candid answers made the short list.

Below are those questions.

1 – How do you feel when you enter campus each day?

2 – How is your home life, place of worship, neighborhood, role models—different or the same from what you see at school?

3 – What does the school do really well to make you feel at home, comfortable, and welcomed?

4 – What could the school do better to make you feel at home, comfortable, and welcomed?

5 – Is there an incident/event you would like to share about your time on campus? A positive interaction with a teacher or student? Or maybe an incident that evoked a sense of feeling like an outsider.

With a team in place, Cathy spent most of January and February directing her film. As the quiet observer, I witnessed interviewees open up about being on financial aid, taking the public bus for two hours, feeling different due to her religious practices, being outspoken in class about conservative political views and feeling like the minority, being embarrassed each time she needed extended time for a test, having to go home and act as interpreter for her parents, or the international student who entered as a freshman speaking very little English and now was proud of earning her spot in AP English. Then there were the talks of the two "N" word incidents. Students of all backgrounds had an opinion. Some were angry or disillusioned and several were apathetic. After the filming was over, Cathy often stayed to talk with each student, instilling in each one that they were part of the solution and genuinely thanked them.

One month later, the entire student body gathered in the auditorium for the Diversity Assembly. It was a video that needed no introduction. Lights out, film rolled, and the audience went silent. There was plenty to smile about as Cathy had strategically placed much of the positive sentiments at the front end. Soon, the reality of the footage became uncomfortable, while others parts were extremely painful. It's important to note that the movie was also a source of pride for many of those who had often felt like the outsider on campus. They felt heard and there was power in that. In short, the movie was a mirror into the reality of the campus culture at the time, and it forced everyone to ask the question, "What action can we take to do better and be better?"

That school year, Cathy could have just stayed silent and angry. Instead, she took a stand, took action, and began a string of events that would begin shifting the culture for years to come.

TRUTH:

What Cathy did was set off a slew of actions that followed over the course of the next five years. This project did not shape Cathy as a leader; it simply brought out the leader inside. As the president of the diversity club, Cathy had found her passion. It was the disconcerting events on her school campus where she found her "why," and that "why" fueled her into action.

I don't have to tell you the importance of diversity on college campuses today. This is not to say that colleges want a diverse student body just for the sake of saying they have one. NO! A leader like Cathy is thoughtful *A leader driven by passion is a leader for life.* about her words and savvy about cultural differences. What this "Coolness Project" reveals to the admission committee is Cathy's willingness to engage in tough conversations and her desire to educate, motivate, and cultivate a community that embraces diversity. As a college admission officer, I want her on my campus. A leader driven by passion is a leader for life.

TIP #15

Your Coolness Factor Is When Your Passion Serves A Bigger Cause.

TALE:
Rose-Colored Glasses

Olivia has always known she wants to become a doctor. As her college counselor, what impressed me was all of her service to the local community with a commitment to vision care for kids. I only happened upon this information by thoroughly reading the parent questionnaire, but oddly, Olivia made no mention of this in her own resume.

"Olivia, tell me a bit more of the eye clinics you've coordinated? Your father wrote about it in the parent questionnaire," I jumped right in. She was surprised that I knew, so I treaded lightly but needed to understand that this was her project and not her father's. I peppered Olivia with questions: what *she* did to get the doctors to give up their time, who *she* connected with at Vista Del Mar, how *she* decided which families and organizations to invite, and ended the conversation with WHY she chose this as her mission.

It turns out Olivia's father, Dr. Carson, was an accomplished eye surgeon. When Olivia was 11 years old, she accompanied her father at USC's local health fair for neighboring families. Dr. Carson's eye center performed screening eye exams for hundreds of visitors that day at the center of campus. "What happens now, Daddy," little Olivia asked, and Dr. Carson explained the exam would detect vision problems and then he would encourage the families to see their doctor for a full eye exam and get a prescription for eyeglasses if necessary. "But what if they don't have an eye doctor?" The simple question stumped Dr. Carson, and he replied, "Now that is a very good question, Livy, and I don't think I have a very good answer for you."

For years Olivia continued to escort her father to community events, watch him work, but more than anything, she wanted an answer to her question, "What happens if a child needs glasses but cannot afford them?" In 8th grade Olivia asked her father if she could put a basket in his office for people to donate their old eyeglasses. He agreed but did not know that she went to various offices and did the same. In just one year, she collected over 100 pairs of eyeglasses. Once Dr. Carson recognized her interest, he encouraged her to make a plan, and she later presented in front of eight eye doctors at their home. They agreed that if she could, in fact, coordinate an eye clinic for local families, they would give their time for eye screenings, vision exams, and donate prescription eyeglasses. Six months later, in the spring of her sophomore year, Olivia and the eight eye doctors hosted a small "Rose-Colored Glasses" event at the Home-Safe Child Care Center in West Hollywood. Since that time, Olivia had coordinated four additional clinics, with a pool of 25 eye doctors, worked directly with Vista Del Mar Child and Family Services, and served a running total of well over 800 families.

With a little prodding, Olivia spent twenty minutes describing the clinics with vivid details of her most recent "Rose-Colored

Glasses" event held at Vista Del Mar's 18-acre campus. I can still picture the clinic hosted on the peaceful and spacious lawn in the center of Los Angeles: check-in stations manned with a team of high school student volunteers and eye doctors draped in white coats with their mobile eye equipment, while kids of all ethnicities, wearing shorts and colorful socks, waited in line. Her mission was simple: provide eye exams to the youth in Los Angeles, and for those for whom eyeglasses were recommended, she made sure they were provided for free. Olivia's eyes lit up every time she recounted a story about the kids she met, "Frank was just six years old, Diana loves to read, and Michael had lost his confidence in school." Once she seemed to be out of tales, I asked one last question, "WHY doesn't anyone know that you do this, Olivia?" She looked up at me, "Ms. Colón, it's not about that. It's about the kids."

TRUTH:

This tale touches my heart because I am reminded that, no matter your age, YOU can make an impact on one life and/or an entire community.

At the end of the day, it was Olivia's application and credentials that got her admitted in the Early Decision round at Duke University. Though I was not in the room when the committee made their decision, I can only offer my experience to

When you do what is right, find your inner leader, utilize your passion, then you will indeed leave a legacy. This, my friend, is true leadership.

tell you why I believe she received a "big" envelope, even though she had admittedly lower SAT scores than many of her would-be counterparts. Olivia realized her authentic "why" early in her life and found a way to put it all together. First, she came from parents who simply instilled the value of giving back and Olivia never lost sight of the communities she could impact. Second, she was laser focused on her ultimate goal of becoming a pediatrician, and needed a way to add depth to her resume in the medical field. The genius of combining what Olivia loves to do (serve others) and what she has to do (show evidence of a love for medicine), was what made Olivia an easy admit.

When you do what is right, find your inner leader, utilize your passion, then you will indeed leave a legacy. This, my friend, is true leadership.

CHAPTER 4:
Resources and Final Note

What's cool to you, may not be cool to me, but that's what makes YOU super cool! Over the last few years, we've had so many students admitted to top 100 colleges. It is possible. To hear more examples from students admitted to Harvard, Yale, Princeton, Cornell, U Chicago, and UVA, scan the QR code in the resource section at the back of the book and it will take you to the iTunes listing for my podcast, Destination YOUniveristy. There you can hear directly from: Julia (Episode 147), Emilie (Episode 112), Max (Episode 131), Curtis (Episode 122), Sean (Episode 142), Alexandra (Episode 108), Juliana (Episode 120), Osose (Episode 110) and Ashley (Episode 112). And if you want to become a "Dreamer" you can learn more about Dream College Academy (DCA) on my website, www.drcynthiacolon.com. .

OK, I want to be clear, without being discouraging. Not every student will discover a true passion or leave a legacy by the time they turn 17-years old. This is not a problem. The point of this chapter is to help you take the time to reflect on your own authentic why. So many teenagers are in a rat race collecting certificates of participation like tickets spitting out of a skeeball machine at your local game zone. Do not fall into that trap. Join a club or sports teams because you love it. Sing, dance, build, or serve because it brings you joy. Discovering your authentic reason why you do anything will catapult you to the front of the stack of applications. Just like interest makes interesting applicants, an authentic "why" is usually behind every "Coolness Project." Trust me, authenticity pops off the page and can motivate an admission officer to fight for you.

So now what? High school is not easy. You must always be willing to push yourself to grow and improve. No worries, I've got a plan for that too.

Let's get to it!

CHAPTER 5

YOUR SELF IMPROVEMENT PLAN

CHAPTER 5:
Introduction

There are 5 Ds to avoid talking about in your college application essay: Death, Divorce, Devastation, Learning Difference or an actual "D" on your transcript. I could never quite understand why teenagers felt so drawn to talk about these five topics. It was as if teens are trying to find the worst story possible in their 18 years of living. The devastation part of their story does NOT make for a compelling essay. This is the mistake so many teens make.

If you have lied, cheated, made a mistake, or done something stupid, you are not alone. Welcome to being a scrappy teenager. Admission folks love scrappy way more than the superb.

If you can commit to memorizing the 5 Ds, then you can learn what I call the 25% rule. If you insist on writing your essay on one of these five topics (and sometimes you need to), I strongly encourage you to follow the 25% rule: spend no more than 25% of your essay describing the "D" scenario. Use the remainder of the essay to describe how you grew, what you did, how you overcame, and the lessons learned. THAT is what makes for an interesting, engaging, and compelling essay.

The next tales are not just high school lessons, these are life lessons. In tale #16 we meet Hannah who is under a tremendous amount of pressure to perform academically and makes a fatal mistake during a final exam. Cosette, who you met in tale #1, is rejected from every college in her senior year, her story will inspire you in tale #17. If you've lost a parent like Jeremy, you will need tissue while reading tale #18. In tale #19, it is me, yours truly, who pouts after being denied a spot on the newspaper staff. Tale #20 calls on us to think about what we would do when faced with the choice to do what we want to do versus doing the right thing. Craig is faced with just that choice.

Now, before you go thinking you can skip this chapter, hold the phone. Nobody, and I mean nobody is perfect. If you have lied, cheated, made a mistake, or done something stupid, you are not alone. Welcome to being a scrappy teenager. Admission folks love scrappy way more than the superb.

Even if you select one or two tales from this section, I guarantee you will learn something new about yourself and the college admission process.

Now, let's get to it!

| TIP #16 | The Bigger The Mistake, The Greater The Comeback. |

TALE:
Making Lemonade Out Of Lemons

Her khaki pleated skirt shifted from side to side as she took her assigned seat in the library. Two and a half hours later, Hannah was one of the last students to exit. "Have a good day, ladies," Mrs. Jones said good-bye to Hannah and the two others. Mrs. Jones took one last sweep around the private stalls and stopped at a curious folded piece of paper left on the back right hand corner of the wooden armed library chair. Mrs. Smith unfolded the paper and realized what it was: a cheat sheet for the final exam in the chair Hannah had just occupied.

At the end of the following day, I invited Hannah to my office with the junior counselor, Ms. Eaton, present. With my standard first question, I began, "Do you know why you are here?" In this case, Hannah answered with a simple, "No." I explained what was found in her chair just one day earlier, showed her the paper without handing it to her, and asked her to tell me about it. I was pleased when Hannah began to explain her situation. While she did not deny that it was her piece of paper, she did deny using it during the final exam. Tears welled up as she described, "Ms.

Colón, the pressure is so much. I have to keep up with volleyball and my grades. I have to get into a good college." I stared back at her—into those deep brown eyes, "But Hannah, what I don't understand is that you were doing well in this class." She went into the final exam with an A-, a perfectly acceptable grade. "I know, I don't know why I doubted myself," she claimed it was a security blanket, that even though she knew the material, she wanted to ensure an A on the exam. Unfortunately, from my vantage point, Hannah was about to earn an F on her US History final, which would move her coveted A- down to at least a straight B.

The next day Hannah returned to hear the "verdict" in a second meeting that now included her parents. Suffice to say everyone was remorseful of the obvious mistake, supportive of Hannah, and ready to accept the consequences. Truth be told, this was not what I was expecting. The pressure of athletics and school that Hannah had described the day before often comes from home; one or both parents that have ingrained into their child's head that nothing less than the best will do. I did not find that in this set of parents, and I was so pleased that their response was to support Hannah while accepting the decision of the school. Their willingness to view this mistake as a stumble, instead of a catastrophe, played a key role in how Hannah would ultimately handle her situation. The verdict included a four-day in house suspension to begin when we returned in January.

As a junior, Hannah could have decided her life was over; however, this scholar athlete was determined to keep moving forward. Part of her four-day suspension was to meet with me for the last 30 minutes of school. I mentored her, and on the third day I planted a seed about starting an honor council, "You know, the Head of School has always wanted the students to own the discipline process." The next day Hannah came bounding into my office with a binder of researched honor councils from around the country. She became obsessed with creating an honor council for her school. Hannah's proposal to the Head of School was approved and soon an interim group of 12 students, led by Hannah, produced a constitution, voting procedures, and elections by spring of the following year. In her college essay, she recounted her efforts of becoming one of the 12 founders of the honor council. I'm proud to say, Hannah was admitted to her first choice school, Emory University.

TRUTH:

Resist the notion that you must become the ideal applicant. I read 25-35 admission files per day, and pretty and perfect was sometimes boring. Life is simply not that easy, nor free of challenges along the way. Some of the most interesting essays were those stories where the applicant recounted a stumble, great or small, and their decision to get up, try again, push forward, and not allow the past to determine their future. Once she owned her failure, Hannah was determined to make amends with all of those she disappointed, including herself.

Equally important to Hannah was her wish to teach other students that they too should always believe in their own knowledge and not resort to cheating.

Whether her motivation to start the honor council was purely altruistic or not does not matter. What matters here is with nearly zero recovery time, Hannah dusted herself off and found a way to turn her lemons into lemonade. Some students feel embarrassed after even the smallest of mistakes and then shy away from the adults in their life. While others live in denial and pretend it never happened. Neither of these strategies are good ones, nor should you entertain your desire to ignore the situation.

Don't let a stumble get you down, find a way to make lemonade.

TIP #17

A College Rejection Is The Best Motivation To Finally Figure It Out.

TALE:

The California Dream Is Delayed For Two Years.

Cosette just sat staring off into space. Her favorite navy worn-in sweatshirt bore the gold letters UCSB. Her family had traveled to California the summer before senior year, and Cosette knew it was the perfect place to study. She found inspiration on hikes in the mountains, but equally enjoyed the expansive views of the ocean. In September she had gone to the college counseling office, only to learn how competitive it would be for Cosette to access a UC campus as an out-of-state applicant. In her seventh semester at Our Lady of Good Counsel, she regretted not pushing herself to study just a bit more and challenge herself with a more rigorous curriculum. Cosette could not bear to tell her friends that she had been denied at her dream college.

Cosette was the perfect "solid" student. She had an equal number of As and Bs and a sprinkling of honors and one advanced placement course in senior year. As a member of the Treble Choir, she was clearly a talented singer. Of the nearly 3000 4-year colleges in the US, Cosette would easily be admitted to 90% of that list. Had she listened to her counselor, Cosette would have been admitted to St. Mary's College in Maryland and Goucher College. Instead, she had nothing to show for. It was on this sunny April day when Cosette would break the news to her gal pals.

Molly, Christine, and Sheetal rallied around and gave her a great big group hug. Cosette's big brown eyes could no longer hold back the tears. The girls knew there was nothing they could say to console her, so they all sat in silence, protecting their long time friend.

It would take Cosette another year to finally figure out what she was doing wrong. As a senior she applied to college as an art major, yet her resume was filled with music and singing. When she reapplied to college as a transfer student just months into her first year at Community College, she was rejected again by all the same colleges. It was then that she understood the need to change her study habits, improve her grades, and prove to her dream colleges that she was indeed ready for the challenge of academics.

By the end of her first year in college, Cosette had earned a 3.9 GPA. Seven As and one A minus. Her mother had never been so proud, not because of the As, but because Cosette made a decision to change her future.

Cosette had books about the story of Walt Disney and about animation that had been collecting dust on her bedroom bookshelf. It was during the pandemic that she began to follow what had been her calling all along. Mrs. Jae Perez, the art teacher in high school had always praised her drawings and now Cosette would do the unthinkable. TikTok became all the rage and Cosette decided to animate Aladdin's Genie to dance. Cosette spent three months creating 144 animation slides to yield a 17 second TikTok video. Let me repeat, she spent three months creating 144 animation frames that lasted a total of 17 seconds. I don't know about you, but I would have given up after slide number four. WOWZA! Once I learned this fact about Cosette, I knew she was determined to get admitted to the college of her choice.

TRUTH:

The truth is this: NOBODY can do the work for you. At some point, you have to realize that your grades are only half of the story, but a necessary part of the puzzle. Once you get your academic house in order, your mind will be freed up to figure out exactly who you are, what you are really good at, and find the major and the colleges that are perfect for YOU.

It took courage for Cosette to go through high school and again through the first year of community college and be rejected again and again. However, she knew that a denial was not the end of the road. She had faith that she would figure it out, and for Cosette, Christmas came in April two years after her senior year. Not only was she admitted to Chapman University, Loyola Marymount University, and her dream school, UCSB. Cosette found herself in a pickle when she was also admitted to UC Berkeley.

Once you get your academic house in order, your mind will be freed up to figure out exactly who you are, what you are really good at, and find the major and the colleges that are perfect for YOU.

On her visit to Los Angeles, we finally met in person. Cosette was just as tiny as I am, 5 feet tall on a good day. We hugged and celebrated over Mexican food when she announced that she would be headed to the Bay area and study at Berkeley. I cried, not because of her choice, but because for the first time in nearly one year, I finally saw her teeth. Her smile beamed across her face and I couldn't help but cry and laugh at the same time. Go Bears!

TIP #18 — Life After The Death Of A Parent Takes Time. Advocate For Yourself.

TALE:
The Tempest in the Garden

I met Mr. Swanson in September at the national college fair in Minnesota. Dressed in khaki pants and a navy golf polo, Mr. Swanson immediately asked about the 9-hole course on campus followed by a question about the Shakespeare Garden. Impressed with his knowledge, I gushed about both, "The Garden is absolutely my favorite spot on campus." A young man joined us as he moved from the Vanderbilt display to Vassar, "This is where Mom went to college," Mr. Swanson shared with his son. I smiled at the six-foot tall teen and continued, "The golf course is open to the public, but students can play a round for $2." Mr. Swanson paused a moment before filling in the silence, "This is my son, Jeremy, he plays golf and soccer." I shook Jeremy's hand before he sauntered off to visit Villanova's table. Mr. Swanson completed an information card, now officially adding Jeremy to our mailing list.

> *Almost every teenager has something that feels like a barrier to success.*

Over the course of the year, I received three email messages from Mr. Swanson noting Jeremy's soccer or golf accomplishments, and he never failed to include an academic highlight. At the close of April and all the admission festivities, I prepared for spring travel, which would take me back to the Twin Cities. "Case Studies" was an annual event put on by a collection of six schools for all junior families. Having read four sample college applications, students and parents were paired with two admission officers and given the task of voting on which applicants would be admitted, wait-listed, or denied.

At the end of the evening, Mr. Swanson stopped in to say hello, "I have been wanting to talk to you about . . ." his words lingered in the air when Jeremy interrupted. "Thank you for coming tonight. I found it very informative. This process makes me nervous." Jeremy's name badge denoted him as an Ambassador and just as Mr. Swanson tried to continue our conversation, Jeremy jumped in to ask about the biology and environmental studies majors on campus.

"Jeremy, why don't you tell Cynthia about your sophomore year."

"I will, Dad, but not now."

I continued to pack up my display while in the middle of a family argument.

"Jeremy, now is as good of a time as any."

"I will, I know. Please, Dad. Not now."

Jeremy had been assigned to help me to my car with any display items or boxes. "Is everything OK, Jeremy?" I inquired. "Yes, my father is worried about my dip in grades in spring of sophomore year. But I assure you, my transcript is flawless this year." I thanked him and gave him my business card.

It would be eight months before I heard from Jeremy again, this time through the one vehicle he had to advocate for himself, his college essay.

I wanted to see Shakespeare Garden. That was the only reason I chose the college trip to New York. Sitting on the bench surrounded by the newly bloomed pansies, I was angry. Why wasn't she the one to bring me here? I wanted my mother to be the one to show me her garden she loved so much. Rushing from soccer practice late October I did not make it to the hospital in time. How could she leave me? Why did I argue with her the night before? I had left the house that morning without an "I love you," or even a "Have a good day." And then she was gone. Just like that. No notice. No warning. No more hugs. I would never forgive myself.

I have no recollection of the rest of sophomore year. I was a zombie, going through the motions of school and yet clearly unaware of my surroundings. The sympathetic looks from teachers only made me despise myself even more. I did not deserve their sympathy; I was a terrible son.

Though I could not speak, that spring, I planted pansies, daisies, and marigolds. I carefully followed the geometrical patterns Mom had laid out. Dad and I added a mulberry tree with a bench underneath, just like Mom had described.

That spring I traded in my golf clubs for rakes, forks, and spades. Instead of putting, I found myself pruning the garden; guiding, directing, and shaping. With her garden intact, there were days I thought she just might return.

Today, I am no longer that Tempest in the Garden. With each year, the garden blooms more fully and vibrantly, as does my soul.

I could not hold back the tears. It all finally made sense. Jeremy's grades had taken a tumble in sophomore year because of the tragic and unexpected death of his mother. Until now, he had not been able to make sense of what happened, much less find the words to advocate for himself.

TRUTH:

This is a story about a dad trying diligently to advocate for his son, and at the same time, this is a tale about Jeremy coming into his own, making peace with his life's challenges, and eventually advocating for himself. Jeremy understood very clearly that it was his job to explain his dip in grades and not his father's story to tell. He just needed time.

Whatever barriers are in your way, I encourage you to prune them and shape who you are. And when you do, you will shine!

Consider your obstacles. Almost every teenager has something that feels like a barrier to success. Sometimes it is a known barrier, like with Jeremy, and others suffer from low self-confidence, a tough home life, depression, or a learning difference.

Colleges want fighters, students who have the wherewithal to keep moving forward, and those who are willing to advocate for themselves. Whatever barriers are in your way, I encourage you to prune them and shape who you are. And when you do, you will shine!

TIP #19

You Don't Always Win.
Eat Ice Cream Anyway.

TALE:
Like A Blade Of A Sword,
Rejection Pierces The Heart

Cyndie stood over the round receptacle tearing the official letter piece by piece in front of the very teacher who had issued that letter. As the bell rang, Mrs. Rosenberg raised her voice just a bit, "Everyone, take your seats." Making her statement known, Cyndie continued tearing her notice until she could not tear anymore. With a flip of her cheer skirt, she walked away from her otherwise front row seat. Cyndie was in no mood to raise her hand in English class. Today was not her day. Kristin knew not to say anything, but in support of her best friend, she too sat at the back of the room for the first time all year.

Kristin and Cyndie became quick friends when they were the only two rising freshmen to make the junior varsity cheer team. Since then, they had been inseparable. Cheer team led to joining the Key Club and later that fall they ran for class council and won. Early in the spring semester, Cyndie took a job as a hostess at the local family-owned restaurant and often left school immediately to make her 4 p.m. shift. Cyndie encouraged Kristin to join the school newspaper and take photos at the after-school events.

Sophomore year, the two continued to conquer the world of high school. In addition to the long hours on campus for co-curricular activities, the two succeeded in honors classes. Kristin tried acting and landed a role in the fall play and spring musical. Cyndie found her niche on the soccer and softball fields. And somehow they always had time for each other before school, at lunch, and on the weekends.

Popping open the tab of her Dr. Pepper, Kristin suggested, "You know, you should apply for the junior staff spot for 'The Blade.' We're going to need new writers for next year."

Cyndie opened her mini chocolate donuts and offered one to Kristin, "Yeah, I thought of that, but I'm not a writer."

Picking one out of the sleeve, Kristin took a bite of her mini-donut and paused to remind her best friend of the most important fact, "Cyndie, you would finally have a reason to attend all the games to root for Scott instead of pretending you're there with me." Cyndie nearly choked on her not-so-mini donut and, with that, she decided to apply.

Cyndie needed a writing sample and ruffled through old papers to find one. "Ah . . . this is perfect," she thought. One of her favorite assignments came from the unit on *Catcher in the Rye*. Ms. DeMuro requested students write a short story using the vocabulary words and keep the character, Holden's, style and diction in mind. Cyndie could not have found a better piece to represent her gifts in writing.

A week later, the bell rang signaling the end of first period, and Cyndie found Kristin among the cackles of high school teens.

"I just got my letter five minutes ago," Cyndie's smile showed her big teeth, "but I wanted to wait for you to open it."

"Well, crazy girl, open it!!"

Emblazoned across the top left hand corner of the white envelope were the words "The Blade" in a crimson-colored stamp. The BHS Buccaneer mascot wore maroon and gold with his arms folded across his chest, sharpened blade in hand.

With a quick tear across the top, Cyndie began to read, but within seconds she stopped and folded it back up.

"I didn't get it. Let's go have lunch," Cyndie was terse in her words and began walking away.

"What do you mean? What does it say?" Cyndie kept walking without a word.

"This must be a mistake, let me read it. Cyndie. Please." Kristin poured over every word twice.

"Two slices of pizza, fries, chocolate donuts, and a Dr. Pepper," this was quite a lunch for Cyndie.

"It says you can apply again early next year, and . . ."

Cyndie interrupted, "Forget it, I'm not good at writing. That's your thing."

They sat in silence sharing donuts and Doritos before Mrs. Rosenberg's class. That week Cyndie's mini-tantrum tainted her otherwise *perfect* reputation, but it made Kristin love her all the more. In solidarity, Kristin joined Cyndie in outwardly pouting for three days in class. By the end of the week Kristin convinced Cyndie to not take her anger out on Mrs. Rosenberg, and, more than that, to stop beating herself up.

That night, Cyndie's dad took the two peas in a pod out for ice cream. "You both amaze me. Between the two of you, you have nearly tried everything at school. I am proud of you."

With two pink spoons in hand, Cyndie and Kristin dug into their polka dot ice-cream cups.

TRUTH:

Rejection is a necessary part of life. The important takeaway from this tale is this—take your time to pout and be mad, but then it is time to get over yourself. You are not the only one who fails, or gets rejected, or did not make the team, or doesn't write perfectly, so stop feeling sorry for yourself. It is important to learn the lesson early in life that you cannot always win everything. Learn to have a good attitude in the face of rejection. These are the best days to go directly to your happy place and make a list on your phone,

If you can learn that trying and failing is part of the journey to your own success, then you won't take the failure so personally.

computer, or on your bedroom wall of all of your accomplishments. Give yourself a gold star for each of them, and I promise you will feel better. If you can learn that trying and failing is part of the journey to your own success, then you won't take the failure so personally.

Never beat yourself up. Learn the lesson rejection is teaching you. And, when in doubt, eat ice cream!

TIP #20

Cheating Doesn't Ruin Your Reputation, It Defines Your Character.

TALE:
Fall From Grace

Once Ken finished his test, he requested permission to go to his locker. Seated next to the now empty desk, Craig took front and back photos of Ken's exam with his phone on silent. By the end of the day, five other juniors received Craig's photos. Thursday afternoon, one of those juniors turned herself in for having cheated on her make-up exam that morning.

"But I did not cheat. I completed my own exam, Mr. Dixon," the junior pleaded his case. Craig McGraw was the pride and joy of his family, a football dynasty. His grandfather, father, and uncle had all played as Varsity Vikings and won state titles in three different decades. Craig had made it his mission for Viking football to return to glory.

As a teenager, you might believe you are invincible, unstoppable, and irreplaceable; and while this may be true for you, proceed with caution.

"But I have seen that the original text came from your phone,"

Craig could hear the disappointment in Mr. Dixon's voice.

"Mr. Dixon, I swear, I know I made a mistake with the photos, but I did not cheat on my exam," Craig's face became beet-red, his heart pounding.

Lesson: Cheating is a choice, not a mistake.

Mr. Dixon had been Craig's freshman football coach and knew then he was destined for greatness. He did everything to contain his heartbreak, "McGraw, tell me right now, what is the academic honor code?" Without hesitation, "I will neither give nor receive aid," Craig lowered his head. "I'm sorry, Coach. I was wrong."

Lesson: Do what is right, not what is easy.

Craig waited in the office while Dean Dixon called Mr. McGraw and scheduled time to meet with me in the principal's office the next morning.

The Vikings were scheduled to play Friday night against a team with a winning record and two seniors already recruited to play Division I college football. Early on in the season, Head Coach Biff (nicknamed for having played at University of Michigan) and Athletic Director, Carlton Ross, knew that a good fight against this team would prove the Vikings were on the rise. This was the game Craig had waited for all year and his entire extended family planned to watch from the bleachers. A Viking team without the star outside linebacker would make it difficult to hold their offense, let alone have a chance of winning.

At six in the evening, Coach Biff and Carlton tapped on my door, and with a nod, they walked in, "What can I do for you, gentlemen?"

"Doc, the whole team is talking about McGraw..." Coach Biff was a bit heated and Carlton jumped in with a different approach.

"This is about the team, the alumni, and the long-term success of Viking football. We simply want you to keep this in mind," Carlton kept it brief and paused.

I probed, "And if a player circulated photos of your secret plays to another team, would you allow him to play at the next game?"

"With all due respect, Doc, that's not the same. Craig says he himself did not cheat on his exam."

"What Coach means is, we don't disagree that he did something wrong. We just believe a suspension can wait until Monday," Carlton's plea offered an alternative to an inevitable scenario.

"Yes, gentlemen, I hear you, and I'll wait to hear directly from Craig in the morning when his father is present. I remind you that lessons on the field are not the only lessons we teach."

Lesson: Success without integrity is failure.

Mr. Dixon arrived early Friday morning and together we agreed on an appropriate plan based on the values of the institution.

I walked out to the lobby and greeted the two men equal in size and stature. "Please, have a seat. I think you know Mr. Dixon," everyone shook hands and nestled into their positions. "Craig, I would like you to begin by sharing in your own words what happened."

Silence hung in the air, "Dr. Colón, I am so sorry. My actions do not represent who I am. I have let down my team, my family, and myself." Craig took a deep breath as he was about to say the most painful words in his life. Mr. McGraw placed his hand on his son's back, "I'm here, I'm proud." Those words gave Craig the courage to continue, "I would like to accept my consequence of a suspension today and take myself out of the game."

**Lesson: Your beliefs don't make you a
better person, your behavior does.**

TRUTH:

One of my favorite high school coaches, Ed, used to say, "Football is the biggest thing in *your* life, but it is not the biggest thing *in* life." This tale is a good case in point. We all make mistakes, adults included. But when you fall, the point is to get up, accept consequences, and proceed with integrity. As a teenager, you might believe you are invincible, unstoppable, and irreplaceable; and while this may be true for you, proceed with caution. Understand that not only is it a good thing to fall, but it is encouraged. If you can fall with grace, the life lessons will far outlast those learned in any one season of play.

With regards to college admissions, this is one of those lessons that may never get retold. Craig's athletic prowess would eventually land him a spot on a Division I football team. But I have to believe that it was his humble disposition and character that showed through every time Craig met a new college coach that eventually afforded him multiple offers. After that incident as a junior, Craig became attentive to his studies and had a nearly perfect record (excluding math class) in his junior year. At the young age of 16, Craig had found a way to fall from grace with humility.

CHAPTER 5:
Resources and Final Note

Did you not love those tales and life lessons? It is truly my favorite chapter, as I believe failure is the perfect ingredient needed for any teen to find the courage necessary to push forward and ultimately, succeed. Chapter 5 is a reminder of just how amazing each of you are. And speaking of amazing, some of our students have overcome obstacles of their own, be it academic or one of the 5 Ds. If you'd like more examples, scan the QR code in the resource section at the back of the book and it will take you

Just like Monday Morning Quarterback is meant to criticize actions and decisions of the past, I claim Self-Improvement Sunday. Get your team of supporters, village of cheerleaders, and community of believers and revise and adjust your plan to win!

to the iTunes listing for my podcast, Destination YOUniveristy. There you can hear directly from: Cosette (Episode 121), Diego (Episode 97), Caroline (Episode 90), Grace (Episode 92), Savannah (Episode 94), Ethan L. (Episode 106), Steve (Episode 95), John (Episode 128) and Jeffrey (Episode 129).

Consider high school one huge tight rope with the biggest safety net underneath. That net is just waiting for you to fall and bounce right back up. You are resilient.

Just like Monday Morning Quarterback is meant to criticize actions and decisions of the past, I claim Self-Improvement

Sunday. Get your team of supporters, village of cheerleaders, and community of believers and revise and adjust your plan to win!

You are now in the home stretch and ready to take control of senior year. You got this!

Let's get to it!

CHAPTER 6

YOUR SENIOR YEAR PLAN

CHAPTER 6:
Introduction

OK, I'm just going to say it, college applications are like taxes for teens. You have to track down transcripts and official documents, report any altruistic giving, fill out the right forms, meet the looming deadline and await a hopeful positive result. This stressful process can take a toll on even the happiest of families.

If you've followed the plan, by September of senior year, ninety percent of the heavy lifting is over. All that is left to do is put all those puzzle pieces together, complete the forms, and hit submit. This chapter offers a step-by-step process for building your list of colleges, how to choose your essay topic, and how to ask for teacher letters of recommendation.

Before we dive in, I'm going to give you a list of To Dos.

MUST DOS:

1 – Treat applying to college as a temporary part time job and carve out time every single week dedicated to working on applications.

2 – Find at least 15 minutes per day to jump, run, paint, sing, or scream to relieve stress.

SHOULD DOS:

1 – Begin working on applications and gathering data the summer before senior year.

2 – Schedule a weekly 40-50 minute meeting with your parents/mentors. This will prevent them from peppering you with daily questions.

COULD DOS:

1 – Find an essay coach. That might be your English teacher, school counselor, my YouTube videos or free essay samples, or you might sign up for an essay camp. Whatever you do, find someone who understands that a college essay is different from an English assignment.

Now, let's get to it!

TIP #21 — Your List Of Colleges Is Key. The Goal Is To Have Choices In April.

TALE:
Listen To Your Counselor,
Then Choose What's Right For You

Saige was a solid B student, with a couple of advanced placement courses, average test scores, and a decent list of activities. Just last week, Saige walked into my office and in all seriousness said, "Ms. Colón, I decided I want Dartmouth." A kid like Saige could access nearly every four-year college in the country, just not the highly selective ones. As I waited for her arrival, I was armed with several colleges to add to her list.

"I know you want to discuss your early application to Dartmouth, so we can do that first. Then I want to discuss your list of colleges. Sounds good?"

"Sure. I have a list that I brought," Saige pulled out a sheet of notebook paper with a list of colleges. I acknowledged the list and left it on the desk while we discussed her writing, water polo, and her work with School on Wheels. I took her smirk as a sign of trust.

"Let's take a look at your list."

Her first list included Duke, Brown, Stanford, Northwestern,

Amherst, Columbia, UC Berkeley, and Vassar.

"Saige, these are all considered Reach schools for anyone. Let's find a range of schools before we finalize. Sounds good?"

For the first time, Saige shifted in her cushioned chair. The remainder of our time was spent in negotiations like two 4th graders exchanging lunch items from their lunch pail, "I'll give you my fudge stripes cookies for your bag of gummy bears."

We needed Realistic Reach schools, as well as 50-50, and Target colleges to round out her list. I suggested adding Oberlin, University of Iowa, Hamilton, Colby, and Emory. Saige stared at my list and began to cross some off the list.

"Saige," I looked directly at her, "My job is to make sure you have plenty of options this April. Your list does not include any slam dunks."

Just before winter break, Saige appeared in the doorframe of my office. Leaned against her left side, her mane of hair hung in the gap between the frame and her shoulder. Her face—plain. Her emotion—sad.

"I was denied," she remained motionless.

I tilted my head to mirror her lean and said, "Oh, Saige, I'm so sorry." She stared through me and slowly pulled herself away from the door and into my office.

"I want to re-apply in 'regular decision'," the moment of comfort was immediately stolen by her matter-of-fact tone.

"Saige, a deny means that they have eliminated you from their applicant pool," as loving as it sounded in my head, there was no way to kindly say those words to a teenager whose dream has just been punched in the face. I sat quietly and let her grieve her loss. It occurred to me for the first time that she *never* saw this coming.

I bumped into Saige after winter break, "How did it go with the applications, Saige? I only received your paperwork for your first choice schools."

"Oh. I didn't apply to the others. I don't really want to go to any of them." I was ill equipped to respond.

"Saige, I don't know that you will get into any of those schools. And now the January 15 deadline is in a week."

Saige shrugged her shoulders as if to say, "It's fine. No need to freak out."

Within five minutes of leaving my office, I printed a Common Application and personally delivered it to Saige in class and insisted she complete the application by Friday. Thursday morning, before the first bell, I had the complete application in hand. Saige had chosen ten schools that I was pleased with, and on her own had discovered Colorado College, Manhattanville, and Wheaton Colleges. Saige was sure to have choices in April.

TRUTH:

There are nearly 3,000 four-year colleges and universities to choose from in the United States alone. Do not, I repeat, do NOT set your heart only on the top 100. Do yourself a favor and go back to chapter two of this book, and do your homework. Be open to new places, and find institutions that have the major you are looking for. Remember, there are three decisions in college

There are nearly 3,000 four-year colleges and universities to choose from in the United States alone. Do not, I repeat, do NOT set your heart only on the top 100.

admissions: 1) Where you apply, 2) Where you get admitted, and 3) Where you enroll. YOU have complete control over two-thirds of this process, but you must begin with a bullet proof college list. Capiche? Listen to your counselor. Counselors often have a suggestion or two that you have never heard of and could be a good match.

THERE IS ONLY ONE MUST DO:

Your only job in the application process is to ensure you have choices. In order to do that you must follow my instructions: Be sure to stack your list with no more than 25% Realistic Reach schools, 50% 50-50/Target schools, and 25% Likely/Most Likely schools.

For example, if you are applying to 16 colleges, 4 would be your "dream" schools, 4 would be your safety schools, and 8 would become your 50-50 and Target colleges. Resist the temptation to overestimate your "odds" of getting admitted.

> **TIP #22**
>
> Always Ask For A *Positive* Letter Of Recommendation From Your Teacher.

TALE:

T-A-C: How to get the best out of your teacher!

The summer I spent teaching English to incoming freshmen, I taught them the formula for writing a body paragraph, including a topic sentence, analysis, and a conclusion sentence (T-A-C). I later stole that formula as a college counselor and showed students how they could *If you can take the time to help your teachers, they will go out of their way to give you their best write-up!* consider T-A-C with regards to the letter of recommendations from their teachers, "Thinking about T for the thesis of the letter, A for their argument or supporting evidence, and C as the conclusion paragraph for the admission officer."

Consider for a moment the task of a teacher when s/he sits down to write a letter of recommendation. The teacher may have a great thesis statement but cannot recall the supporting evidence to support her claim. Or he might have one recollection of the fabulous paper you wrote about Madeleine Albright as the first female Secretary of State but has no clue what you do outside of the classroom. We want to avoid this from happening by doing all the work on the front end. I have found the best letters of recommendation come when a student has taken the time to draft up his/her own T-A-C to give to each recommender.

STEP 1:

Reflect on why you are asking this particular teacher to write your letter of recommendation. Most likely you have decided that s/he can highlight your skills in communication, writing, research, visual or performing arts, or math, science, or technology. This teacher might also be able to describe your qualities as a leader, athlete, or community builder. Being clear about what you believe your teacher can highlight is key in acquiring the courage to ask. Giving the teacher even one nugget in your initial request will almost always guarantee that the teacher will respond with an enthusiastic "Yes."

Matthew might say, "Mr. Baran, I was hoping you might agree to write my college letter of recommendation." Breathe. "I learned how to better communicate my arguments through the debates in your class. Do you think you could write a *positive* letter of recommendation about me?"

STEP 2:

After a "yes" from one or two teachers, the hard work follows. Using an abridged version of the T-A-C formula, draft your own short essay about yourself for each teacher. Decide on two or three qualities you would like each teacher to highlight. Giving the teacher specific skills and qualities helps him/her contemplate additional positive examples of their own. It is in the supportive evidence that you can offer a teacher that will ultimately infiltrate their minds as they write your letter. A stand-out letter is one that can convey strong anecdotal evidence to support a teacher's claim. The following are reduced examples:

For Matthew's Social Studies Teacher:

In your American history course, I became a better communicator by learning how to develop stronger arguments among my peers through the debate and discussions in your classroom. I was able to utilize those skills in my final paper, making a persuasive case of why Leroy Robert "Satchel" Paige is the best pitcher in baseball history.

For Matthew's Science Teacher:

Taking an introductory physics course with you as a freshman inspired me to join "Record Sea-ker," the school robotics team. As the moderator of that team, I learned from you how to build, program, and operate a real robot. I remember when "Seas the Day," malfunctioned last year at the FIRST competition. With your guidance, I was able to lead my team to collaboratively diagnose the problem and quickly repair the damage before the next elimination round.

STEP 3:

You are now on your way to getting the best out of your teacher and submitting a quality application. Give yourself a round of applause!

TRUTH:

Not every college requires letters of recommendation. However, for those that do, they matter. Why? Each piece of the application—the transcript, test scores, personal essays, letters of recommendation, and possibly an interview—paints an additional piece of who you are as a student and as a human being. Consider each piece as quilting together the masterpiece of your life that authentically shares the story of you.

The craft of writing takes time and does not come easy for all teachers. If you can take the time to help your teachers, they will go out of their way to give you their best write-up! This exercise shows the teacher that you are professional and are taking the college admission process seriously. Exercise the control you have in all portions of your application, and you will be the better for it.

TIP #23

What You Do Becomes Your Resume. Why You Do It Becomes Your Essay.

TALE:
Find Your Why And Thrive

What do you value? What is important to you? How do you begin to decide what to write about in the most important essay of your life? As your college counselor, I can help with this.

In Essay Bootcamp, we begin with a 15-minute "Values" exercise. We ask students to write down the first things that come to mind within seven categories: People, Places, Leadership, Experiences, Hobbies, Objects, and Work Experiences. Examples include Grandma, family vacation, cooking or film club, comic books, divorced parents, or a sneaker collection. Even at the young age of 15 or 17 years old, there is plenty to write about that will give any reader a real peek into your life. But this takes time and thoughtful reflection.

Once you have decided on your top values (your "WHATs"), in the next column, write down WHY it is important to you. For example, if you value sports, your WHY is likely one of three reasons: 1) the competitiveness, 2) the camaraderie you've found, 3) you are a connoisseur of the sport. These are three completely different essays. In the final column, describe a memory that comes from your WHY column, not your WHAT column. Once you find the perfect memory to go with your why, you are in business!

It is easy to spot an essay from a writer who took the time to find their WHY. These three excerpts below come after several, and I mean more than four, drafts.

JAMES:
Freedom to be Me (summer experience)

Armed with green hair dye and orange tempera paint, we set a date. We met on the grassy quad and 25 kids proceeded to paint my body, head to foot. There I stood, with brown shorts, turquoise curly hair, and orange paint cracking everywhere. Our activity coincided with Water Bottle Bongos and the Meditation Circle. Soon, the three groups merged and formed a chaotic clot of drumming, incense waving, and Jamba Juice sipping kids performing tribal dances and giggling with delight. And in the middle was one Oompah Loompah having the time of his life.

I remember James so well because he was uber smart. He came across as super serious and uncompromising. These qualities made him unapproachable to most of his peers. I was determined to crack him and figure out what makes him tick. His values included, academic decathlon, robotics team, and Center for Talented Youth. My immediate thought was this, "For where he is applying, everyone is smart and has these listed on their resumes. How do we make him come to life on paper?" He began drafting on Monday. After Tuesday's draft, I was still not overly enthused, proving that even the smartest kid in the room can write a dry essay. I took him outside and made him tell me story after story, until he finally cracked a smile. We found it. "Draft that story," I said and he looked puzzled. "Trust me, that is your 'why,'" and he followed my directions. This essay embodies the real James, and at the same time it shows the reader the kind of place James will fit in: where he will discover his people.

RICHARD:
Ice Hockey in LA (athletics)

When my friends and I approached our athletic director, he immediately turned us down. Refused to be defeated, we began looking for a league to join. During this process, we discovered that the local professional team was looking to sponsor a high school hockey league. All we needed was $200 per player, and we would become a member of the league. There were two problems: first, we only had three players, but needed six, and second, we had no money to join.

> ...

We held tryouts, three players showed up, doubled our team, and a starting line up was born.

This is a good example of how sometimes the sport essay is not about playing the sport at all. It was clear when I met Richard that he loved ice hockey but hated that it was not a popular sport in Los Angeles. Richard knew everything, and I mean EVERYTHING, about hockey, and that summer I learned too. But what it boiled down to was how proud he was that he founded the ice hockey team at his school. In other words, his Value/WHAT was clear: Ice Hockey. His WHY was not about playing the sport but leaving a legacy of the sport he loved at the school he loved. The reader comes away from this essay understanding Richard's passion for the sport, his resilience to keep pushing forward, and his leadership qualities among his peers. Brilliant.

AUTUMN'S ESSAY:
Okefenokee Swamp (Travel with family)

The bow of our boat cut slowly through the murky, tea-colored water. The wet bark and lazy branches, bending down as if attempting to drink from the liquid, added to the ancient, mysterious aurora that permeated the swamp. As I looked around the boat, I suddenly remembered I was not living in the middle of a suspenseful and intriguing adventure story, but in the middle of my family's annual road trip.

. . .

Tony, the tour guide, went on to explain that Okefenokee came from the Native American for "land of the trembling earth." Looking around the boat at the faces of my family, the world felt surprisingly stable to me.

This is one of my all time favorite essays. When Autumn and I first began to work together, she had written in her first column, "Traveling to 47 states." When pushed on her "why," she said things like, "seeing the country," "exploring national parks," and "driving in the car for hours with her family." Boom, I thought, there it is. Her eyes lit up when she shared countless tales of her family's summer excursions across the US map from Grand Tetons to Acadia National Parks. Her WHY was not in fact about the thousands of miles she has traveled, but rather, the quality time she spends with her immediate family. This essay is one brief window of time in Autumn's life with her mom, dad, and sister. Jayne paints a clear picture of the kind of adventures she has experienced, but more than that, we understand that she values her incredibly close family.

TRUTH:

The truth is, at 17 years old, you have everything it takes to write a tremendous essay. The key is honing in on why you've chosen the topic. This essay is only one window for the reader of your application to get a glimpse into your life. You cannot fit everything into one essay, so remember to take my advice, "It's not what you value, it's about why you value it."

Many students can get away with writing one main essay for the bulk of their applications. If I'm being honest, most of the students we work with all have at least two or more top 100 colleges on their list. If that is you, pay close attention. My recommendation is that you draft up an arsenal of essays. In our essay workshops and camps, we teach the Core 4 Essays: 1) Who Am I, 2) What Am I Good At, 3) What is Something Cool About Me, and 4) Why Do I Want To Major In X Major. If you have this set of essays, I have found that students are able to use, reuse, and retweak these essays over and over again.

You cannot fit everything into one essay, so remember to take my advice, "It's not what you value, it's about why you value it."

I don't want to scare you but let's do the math for one minute. If you are applying to the University of California system, you will need 4 essays. Private and other public colleges across the country typically require one main essay and then an additional 2-3 supplemental essays. Let's say your list included 2 UC campuses and 8 additional private/public colleges, you will need a minimum of 20 different essays that are 350 words or less, plus one main personal statement that is 500-650 words. Do I have your attention now? I thought so. Do not delay, get started on your essays sooner rather than later!

TIP #24

The Best Essay Topics
Are In You But Not
Always Obvious.
Dig Deep.

TALE:
Dig Deeper And Discover A Gem

School was never a top priority for Oliver. Without digging too hard, Oliver achieved decent grades and seemed satisfied with the results. Instead, he poured his energy into theater and his love of books. Oliver was well read but savvy enough to know that while he was a straight B+ student, he needed an essay to help him stand out, which is what led him to my office.

I began with one of my prompts, "Describe for me what I would find on the walls and in the corners of your bedroom." Confused by what his counselor was asking but willing to indulge me, Oliver began. One wall was adorned with Notre Dame paraphernalia and complemented with an old map of the city of South Bend, prominently featuring the southernmost bend of the St. Joseph River, from which the city derived its name. Embarrassed a bit, Oliver admitted he owned Cubs bed sheets—his mother's and his favorite baseball team. His grandmother taught in the Chicago schools and hosted an annual family gathering at Wrigley Field, hoping against all odds that this was finally the year for the pennant. The long wooden dresser was an exhibit of small and large trophies Oliver had won while playing flag football, soccer, and later for acting competitions. After graduating from Notre Dame and St. Mary's College, Oliver's parents chased their dreams in Hollywood, CA. His mom had some success landing a few cameo roles as friend to Tracey Gold's character on the hit show, Growing Pains. "The top right hand drawer is reserved for all the programs of the plays I've acted in," Oliver smiled, and I thought we might be onto something, but without a beat he continued on with the final wall.

"In the corner, is my father's rocking chair next to the reading wall," his expression told me Oliver had saved the best for last. As a child, Oliver's father sat in the rocking chair before bed and Oliver selected a book. Even today it was Oliver's routine to sit and read each night. The bookshelf stood four feet tall, but the entirety of the exposed wall featured framed photos and postcards that Oliver and his father had

The most compelling essays are not only written well, but the story is unique, told in the student's authentic voice, and holds the reader's attention from start to finish.

collected. Curious, I dug deeper and prompted for more details. On a trip to Los Angeles, Mr. Dvorak took Oliver to his favorite bookstore, Book Soup, on Sunset Blvd. It was there that Oliver found a photograph of his favorite actor, Elijah Wood, reading a book. The photo was taken on the set of *Lord of the Rings*, with Elijah, dressed as Frodo, atop a tree reading the hard back book, *Game of Thrones*. Since that time, Oliver and his father made a habit of scouring bookstores, antique stores, and cathedral gift shops for similar photos. His favorite photo highlighted Walt Disney in a rocking chair with one daughter on each knee as he reads a book to them. I didn't have to prod, he continued describing other readers, Abraham Lincoln, Martin Luther King Jr., Marilyn Monroe, Albert Einstein, Hillary Clinton, Helen Keller, and Muhammad Ali. The collection was like his baseball trading cards. Oliver could name the city, state, date, and location of where he and his father had found each prized possession. It was pure joy to watch him recount each one.

There it was. Oliver had dug deeper than he ever had on any homework assignment. The category—people, the subject/topic—his father, the "why"—passing on the love of reading, the unique story—the photo of Frodo reading on set begins a tradition. Oliver left my office that day certain of one thing, not a single student in the applicant pool could replicate his essay. He dug deep and discovered his personal gem.

TRUTH:

Your college admission essay offers the admission officer a window into your life. Even a poorly written essay (and there are many) can stand out if the story is engaging. However, the most compelling essays are not only written well, but the story is unique, told in the student's authentic voice, and holds the reader's attention from start to finish. If you can carve out the time to take inventory of what stands out in your life as a high school student and what you value, then you are halfway there. Finding a topic is easy, the trick is to find the particular story that is unique only to you. Re-read the previous tale for a writing exercise to follow.

By and large, college essays are typically much too general and quite often are one-dimensional. What I mean by that is that just as movies are formulaic—boy meets girl, girl falls in love, something terrible happens, boy is reunited with his love in the end—college essays can feel the same way. For example, Oliver could have written his essay with this formula: dad reads to him as a child, Oliver falls in love with reading, a bookshelf of used books always reminds him of his father. A good essay, and yet you can see how by just digging a little deeper, there are layers and dimensions of Oliver we can gain by revisiting, revising, and revamping his essay for several drafts.

No pressure, but this is likely the most important essay you will write in your life thus far. Do not settle for one-dimensional. Do not settle for the first or second draft; push yourself to dig deeper.

CHAPTER 6:
Resources and Final Note

If you are in need of good examples of essays, you can go to my website and download a free 10 sample packet. Those essays have stood the test of time! And as for a list of colleges there are so many that I love, some you know and others you may not have heard of—University of Delaware, Fordham, Seton Hall, Agnes Scott, St Louis University, University of Wisconsin and Miami University (OH). If you want to hear about some of my other favorites scan the code in the back of the book: Rice University (Episode 8), Bowdoin College (Episode 43), UNLV (Episode 44), Chapman University (Episode 81), Guilford College (Episode 57), Connecticut College (Episode 4), Evergreen State College (Episode 80), and University of San Francisco (Episode 79).

FINAL NOTE

If you have read this book, made your plan, followed your plan, and adjusted your plan, then your plan is already working. You have given 1000 percent to what you control and now all that is left to do is wait patiently. Go out and enjoy the rest of senior year, you've earned it, and I could not be more proud! Your new plan is around the corner, be sure to celebrate each and every victory long the way.

Let's get to it!

CHAPTER 7

YOUR NEW PLAN AWAITS . . .

CHAPTER 7:
Introduction

Red, Yellow, Green. That's How We Decided Who Got Admitted.

Working in admissions was like being in a constant state of Sophie's Choice. I loved so many students, and most were more than qualified, but at the end of the day, the reality was that we could not admit all of them. My job was to simply evaluate what was on the page. The college application, I realized, was the written form of a job interview for your dream company. Imagine interviewing 25-30 applicants every single day for nearly three months straight. They all begin to sound and look the same. It was the few each day that made me giggle, cry, or simply impressed me with their accolades.

We each voted by holding up a red, yellow, or green index card. Red for deny, yellow for Wait-List, and green for Admit. That's how we decided who got admitted.

I loved every bit of my job except the three weeks of "Committee Days." Every single day in the Kautz House, there were two committees of three admission officers. On the days I led, my stack of files were alphabetized by school and by applicant. One by one, I'd pull out and read my notes from the initial reading and then the committee would fire out questions, clarifications, and one more look at the applicant's senior year curriculum. At the conclusion of my presentation, the room went silent and all that was left to do was vote. We each voted by holding up a red, yellow, or green index card. Red for deny, yellow for Wait-List, and green for Admit. That's how we decided who got admitted.

I still remember Sharon from Palo Alto, CA and Claudia from El Paso, TX who were easy greens right away. Or Jeremy (from Chapter 5) who was first voted a yellow, but later moved to a green. These were the wins, the happy moments of my life as an Admission Officer. But most days were filled with red votes, some that still haunt me to this day. That was no fun.

This chapter is meant to give you hope, while also pulling back the curtain a bit. Every story here ends in victory, but don't be misled. Every single applicant here received at least two letters of rejection or more. And while the sting of rejection pierces through the heart, the badge of courage will always remain. College admissions is not for the faint of heart. It takes incredible courage to put yourself out there to several colleges, knowing very well that each application will result in a red, yellow or green vote. Bravo to you who is willing to be committed and get admitted!

OK, are you ready to see what happened?

Let's do it!

TIP #25

Celebrate Every Big
Envelope As If It Were
The Only One Coming.

TALE:
Big Plans, Big City

Emily was unconventional in her choice of Ivy-type schools. Instead of applying to "H, Y, P" (Harvard, Yale, Princeton), she choose to submit applications to "P, C, C" (University of Pennsylvania, Columbia, Cornell). These three schools were no less powerful, but had the one thing Emily dreamed of since middle school: excellent film programs. The illustrious list of alumni in top entertainment roles made UPenn Emily's top choice, but an acceptance to any one of the triumvirate would surely suffice. Some of her classmates tried talking her into applying to UCLA and USC, but Emily feared the fact that she did not come from entertainment royalty would keep her out of the two best film programs in Los Angeles. From the time she and her parents walked into my office at the young age of 14, Emily was transfixed on the colorful college pennants that decorated the walls. Marymount High School was the perfect place for Emily's big plans and even bigger dreams.

As a freshman, she wasted no time and joined the Spanish

club, became a retreat leader, and found a teacher with an interest in film and founded the film club. Her grandparents surprised her with a gift of two back-to-back spring break trips with Señora Valenzuela. As a sophomore, the group traveled to Costa Rica, where they visited Iguazu Falls. Emily took short video clips at every stop and later edited a short 5-minute film for everyone on the trip. And as a junior, the group

Receiving a big envelope from any college is truly an honor. Celebrate each one as it is the greatest achievement to date. The truth is: it is!

visited five cities in Spain, where Emily insisted on only speaking Spanish for the entire trip and fell head over heels in love with the country. By the time she was a senior, she had perfected her accent and, as the student body president and lead ambassador, she was often asked to speak to groups of 7th and 8th grade girls and/or parents. She always began by saying, "Welcome to Marymount," followed quickly by, "Bienvenidos a todos." Emily's story of her academic growth in the classroom, as a leader on campus, and the opportunities she'd been afforded in the short time at Marymount resonated with so many young girls. Her joyful and genuine disposition won the hearts of everyone she encountered.

As part of the Film Club's spring annual "Shorts on the Lawn," Emily's short 3-minute video featuring her peers dancing in various locations on campus to the tune, "Happy," had become a hit. The admission office used it at events, and it was one of two videos she submitted with her film school applications. The second one told the tale of the ghost of Cantwell Hall, Malory Marone. Emily carefully crafted a tale that spanned generations of women, the story of a young girl's desire to fit in and the risks she took to stand out. The 12-minute short was a delicate balance of the bliss of being a teenager combined with the sting of cruelty among peers. It was perfection—raw, real, and in some ways, rebellious. She won third place at the Los Angeles International Student Film Festival.

Just as we were settling into March, admission decisions began to arrive in the mailboxes and via email. The final week of March, Emily would walk in and hold up her big envelopes and celebrate each and every one. It was no secret that Monday, April 1, was an important day. I arrived early Tuesday morning and waited for Emily in my office. Her big blue eyes and brown bouncy locks entered with a smile, we celebrated the one big envelope and the three small envelopes went unspoken. While P, C, C had decided to pass on Emily, this final big envelope marked her seventh acceptance letter. If Emily was disappointed, sad, or even angry, I wouldn't know it. In my office, she maintained her joyful disposition and we debated among the choices in front of her.

Over spring break, Emily and her parents traveled east to the three schools she had narrowed it down to. The Monday following her trip, Emily showed up with two gifts for me, a soy chai latte, and in the opposite hand she held up an NYU college pennant for my office. "I noticed this one was missing, Ms. Colón," and with that I knew Emily had found her home.

TRUTH :

Every year, hundreds—no scratch that—thousands of students are disappointed, parents are mystified, and even counselors are sometimes at a loss for words over denied decisions that come from above. Yes, we could easily attribute the deny letters to the two Bs Emily earned in her high school career, or the slightly (and I mean slightly) lower test scores, or maybe her glowing "coolness" factor didn't come across on paper. It is natural to want to boil it down to just one thing that prevented the pearly gates from opening, but we will never know. The truth is there is no good answer but to say this, understand that at the very selective colleges there are more qualified students than there are spaces. As hard as rejection is to swallow, remember to celebrate each "big" envelope as though it is the only one coming. If you can do that, then you will see how easy it is to fall in love with any school where you chose to apply and who choses YOU back. Emily wisely chose to fall in love with the college that loved her back.

The college admission process is not always fair. There are several milestones in this process, cherish each and every one of them. Receiving a big envelope from any college is truly an honor. Celebrate each one as it is the greatest achievement to date. The truth is: it is! Congratulations! Now go eat ice cream!

TIP #26   A Wait-List Letter Is
Neither A Yes Nor A No.

TALE:
April Showers Sometimes Bring May Flowers

Though rare, I thought I should shed light on the admission letter known as the "in limbo" letter. You are neither admitted nor denied, you are simply in temporary limbo.

CANDIDATE #1:

Colette applied to only one Ivy League school, Columbia, for her love of their writing program. She had all the numbers, high grade point average, top ranked in her class, high SAT scores, and an 800 on the writing portion of the exam. Colette had given up competing as an Irish step dancer by the end of her sophomore year to dedicate her time to writing. Mrs. Miller had groomed her, and by senior year, Colette was editor in chief of the school newspaper and of the literary magazine. She had found her calling and won accolades for her opinion pieces and poetry. Colette had also recently taken a liking to being part of the tech crew for the performing arts productions. So when she was not working on her novel, you could find her behind the stage. Teachers raved about her and sent great letters of recommendation. Mrs. Miller lauded, "Colette is by far the best student I've had in my 25 year career as a teacher." There is no doubt the only thin envelope that read, "wait-list," was a shot to her ego. Though her desk was filled with acceptance letters from all over the country, this April shower rained hard on Colette's parade.

Collete's response:

As her college counselor, I called the admission office, "Diane, she is one of our finest, is there anything she can do?" Diane offered that her office had seen a huge increase in applicants, and she agreed that just one year before, Colette might not have been overlooked. She gave me hope, and I enthusiastically delivered my message to Colette, insisting she could write a letter reminding Diane (the Los Angeles representative) of why the college was her first choice, her most recent accolades, and how she would become a contributing member of the community. Colette wanted none of it. If they could not see how fabulous she was in the first round, she would not put up a fight. The shot to her ego was the bullet she accepted as her fate. Colette thanked me for my encouragement but went on to become a Wildcat at Northwestern in Chicago.

CANDIDATE #2:

William Friedman was from Scarsdale, New York, and attended a beautiful, sprawling campus. At first glance, William did not seem to fit the typical liberal arts applicant; he played football every fall and lacrosse in the spring. His most recent summers were spent in the city with coveted internships with Citicorp and CBS and wrote about his experiences in his essays. His desired major was listed as economics. William was definitely a student Vassar wanted, but compared to his private school counterparts, there were others who ranked higher and showed more compelling reasons why they were a fit for our college. To add complexity to our decision was the reality of where William's parents went to school. While there was no chance of William attending Wellesley College, where his mother attended, William's father attended Brown and worked as a senior partner at McKinsey & Company.

You cannot afford to be humble in this process; this is the one time you have permission to boast about yourself.

Nearly every applicant in Vassar's pool also applied to Brown, and William was certainly no exception. At the end of the day, our office bet on the likeliness that his legacy status at Brown would win him an acceptance letter, and William would ultimately choose to follow in his father's footsteps. He received a wait-list letter from Vassar.

William's response :

What was not apparent was the fact that Vassar was indeed William's first choice. "Billy," as he preferred to be called, had followed his father's advice in academics and co-curricular choices. Instead of football, Billy longed to be on stage, had finally quit lacrosse and was currently in the spring musical. Billy planned to major in economics while also being part of the performing arts department. After receiving his thin envelope, Billy wrote the most incredible letter to our office with a new unfolding of who he was, who he aspired to become, and how he would learn from his peers at Vassar. Whatever held him back from sharing his true passions in his application was now set free. It was clear that Billy was not his father and now I had a reason to fight for him. Before the end of May, Billy was offered and accepted his spot at Vassar.

TRUTH:

Each year, the landscape of admissions for any given college is different and cannot be predicted. I remember one year we had room to admit nearly 20 students off the wait-list. On the other hand, one year we were over enrolled by early May and could not take a single candidate off the wait-list. With this in mind, understand that a wait-list is not a no, it is, however, a no until further notice.

YOU are your own presidential candidate. It is your job to give the voter, in this case, the admission officer, a *compelling* reason to say, "Yes! I'm voting on her/him." My emphasis here is on the word compelling. As the applicant, this is your chance to be authentically you and at the same time, persuasive.

If you can consider every application as though the institution had only one vote (no matter how selective the college), this should be motivation enough to create the most convincing application you can. It could mean the difference between getting admitted or wait-listed. In either case, you cannot afford to be humble in this process; this is the one time you have permission to boast about yourself. My hope for you is that you will not have to wait until May to bring your well deserved flowers. So make a strong case, and you will earn your big envelope in April.

TIP #27

Choosing A College Is Your Decision, Not Your Parents' Choice.

TALE:
A Darker Shade Of Scarlet

"Shall we flip a coin?" I smugly suggested. Bobby dwelled upon his decision for over a week. "How about rock, paper, scissors," my jokes were no longer funny, and he simply wanted someone to put him out of his misery.

"Come on, Dr. Colón, I need your help." Bobby was desperate, and so I used an exercise I often used with the girls at Marymount. I drew three columns and made four rows. Across the top I listed the two Big 10 schools Bobby was deciding between, and asked, "Should we list one more for good measure? How about my favorite LA school?" Bobby agreed and for the first time in two weeks he cracked a joke, "Well at least I know

I know that telling your parents that their alma mater is not your first choice, or worse, that it is the last choice on your list, is not easy. Find a moment to be up front and honest about where your heart is and why.

I'll be wearing a shade of red one way or another."

I asked Bobby to list the things that were most important to his college experience. He quickly rattled off, "Business major, sports medicine for student interns, opportunity for study abroad, and school spirit." Each of these was transcribed into the rows on my left. Bobby's job was to rank each school by the criteria on the left.

"Now, of the four criteria you gave me, rank them in order of importance to you," I didn't really have to ask, at his core, Bobby could not wait to major in business. In addition, Bobby led St. Bernard's sports medicine program and "lived" on the field for every home and away game. He read books on the bus rides, completed homework in between games, and was up until one in the morning nearly every school night.

Bobby wanted nothing more than to continue his work on the sidelines, like his father, Michael Thompson, did in college. Bobby's big plan was to double major in business economics and exercise science as an undergraduate and later attend a top business school and become a sports cap analyst for one of his favorite NFL or MLB teams. Bobby's grandfather, known as "Papa Jack," spent his career as the medical doctor for the Cleveland Browns, while his grandmother, "Grandma (Mi)Chelle" worked in the ticket office for Cleveland Indians after she raised the twins, Michael and Mary. When Bobby's father told stories of his childhood, Bobby couldn't imagine a better life than "living" on a field.

Staring at the yellow pad of paper, Bobby knew in an instant the calculation I was about to make. Multiply the column ranking by each of the criteria ranking. For example, Bobby ranked business as his most important factor, earning the row labeled

"Major" as No. 1. Across the row were columns A, B, C, which happen to be listed in order that Bloomberg Businessweek ranked the best undergraduate business schools; therefore, Kelley School of Business earned a 1, Max Fisher College of Business earned a 2, and Marshall School of Business earned a 3.

His heart raced, "Wait, the school with the lowest score is where I should go, not the highest, right?" Bobby's logical and analytical brain beat me to the punch. With a nod from me he stood and paced the floor, "But Papa Jack wants me to go to Columbus and continue the family legacy. I'll never make it on the field as a freshman. Football is too big there. I want hands-on experience on the field." It was as close to him saying, "I don't want to go there," as I had heard from Bobby in nearly a full year. I knew what his top choice was and so did his gut; his logical brain was finally catching up.

"So what are you saying, Bobby?" I waited in silence for his decision.

"I'm going to be a Hoosier!" He smiled the biggest smile and gave me a high five!

Bobby went on to have a grand time every season with football, basketball, and baseball. Papa Jack, Grandma Chelle, and his parents all traveled with Bobby whenever possible. They all proudly wore crimson and cream. Bobby discovered that his very own field of dreams was just a darker shade of scarlet.

TRUTH:

When I was recruited for Vassar College, I presented to rooms filled with students and parents. One of my favorite jokes to tell was that the list of colleges you are applying to often (if not always) contained the colleges where your parents attended at the top of the list. The nervous laughter in the room always told me that I was correct. I gently reminded parents that they had their turn in college, and now this was their child's future at hand. And with that piece of advice, students, like you, exhaled. I am giving you permission to say, "I want to choose what is best for me."

I know that telling your parents that their alma mater is not your first choice, or worse, that it is the last choice on your list, is not easy. Find a moment to be up front and honest about where your heart is and why. Start with, "I don't want to hurt your feelings. I love your school. I am just not sure it is the right one for me." Or you can always say, "I want to make you proud. I found a school that I know I will love as much as you love your college."

TIP #28

Follow Your Heart—Only You Know Where You Are Headed.

TALE:
Red Wings

Top of the 5th, no outs, and the star pitcher just walked the third batter. Time. Coach, catcher, and infielders huddle up on the mound. Scott waves off the coach with a simple, "I got this." Batter number four takes a few warm up swings as Scott brings his glove and ball close to his chest. In a blink, we hear what sounds like a loud hiccup or short dog bark, indicating "Strike 1." Two more strikes follow in an instant. One out. Breathe. He closes his glove around the ball and "boom," batter number five swings, his bat unscathed. Scott delivers two curve balls and just like that, two outs. Bases still loaded, one more out to go. Breathe. Coach knows what's coming, the four-seam fastball is Scott's specialty, and he has been known to clock nearly 100 miles per hour with his secret touch. Batter number six takes the plate. The umpire squats down and "bang," strike one, followed by an immediate, "boom," strike two. The batter has not swung the bat yet and holds out his hand to take a pause to re-group. The crowd is unbelievably quiet: no movement, no chatter, all eyes on the pitcher. Scott looks back, looks front, and in one sweeping motion, the nine-inch ball with red wings flies off his fingers and punches the back of the catcher's glove. The backspin is too much for the batter. Three outs, no runs, bottom of the fifth, the game is scoreless. Scott went on to pitch the remainder of the game and the Buccaneers won.

It was still early in the season, and as a junior, this was his time to shine. Though Scott received most of the attention in the local papers, he was the kind of kid who always gave "props" to his teammates in nearly every interview.

As a sophomore, Scott was already being heavily recruited by college coaches and winning high praise in the papers. That October, Scott watched in awe as the Minnesota Twins won their second World Series Championship. Two months later, Scott opened his mail on a balmy Christmas vacation day, and there it was—a cream colored card with only one recognizable image. The gold embossed trophy stared at Scott as his index and middle fingers traced over each of the individual pennants. The inside only read this, "Merry Christmas … The Minnesota Twins."

Scott's mom beamed with pride at every game, but at home, she was clear about her expectations; school always came first. If her son could put that much effort into his pitching, surely he could do the same in his studies. Her parenting paid off, and Scott was in the top 15 among our class of 300. Vesta's son was not only being recruited by some of the best colleges around the country. Scouts came from Texas, Rice, Notre Dame, USC, UCLA, and ASU. Scott was not a fan of Texas, nor did he think he would survive the cold of the Midwest. If he had to decide at the end of that perfect-pitched day, it would be a coin toss between UCLA and ASU. Two names: Jackie Robinson and Barry Bonds.

At the end of his junior year, the baseball season came to an end when the Bucs battled an old local rival in the championship game and lost. The loss did not slow down the press and the interest in Scott's career. He was now discussed as a potential draft pick. Scott was well aware of the competitive talent and knew he would not be drafted within the first 20 or 30 rounds; his eye was still on college.

As a senior, Scott committed to Arizona State University, to follow in the footsteps of Barry Bonds and other greats like Reggie Jackson. Scott had one motto, "Win as much as I can and play as long as I am able." In his final year, Scott and his teammates finally won the CIF Championship title. This time, the young

The moral of this story is simple: at the end of the day, you are in control of your destiny and because you have planned it that way, you will have choices.

man in the maroon pinstripes pitched all seven innings, giving up only three hits and one run.

In June, Scott faced a tough decision. Now drafted in the 41st round, he had a choice. To his friends, the choice was obvious; take the scholarship and play ball in four years. Scott was not so sure. At the age of eight, he had fallen in love with a nine-inch round ball with tiny red stitching. It is the raise of the 88 inches of waxed red thread that acts as wings each time it rolls from the fingers of a talented pitcher—flying over 90 miles per hour. The euphoric feeling Scott gained each time the ball left his fingertips kept him coming back for more. For Scott, the obvious choice had been clear for ten years.

The gold and maroon ASU college pennant that now hung in his bedroom would soon be replaced with a red and blue pennant that bore the recognizable logo, "Twins."

TRUTH:

If you shoot for the moon, you will land on your star. Your star is unique, and only you know when you have found your home. Choosing a path to explore professional baseball, culinary arts, a career in dance, or design school, is just as impactful to your life's journey as going to college.

Scott did everything right. He followed an academic plan, athletic plan, and leadership plan. The moral of this story is simple: at the end of the day, you are in control of your destiny and because you have planned it that way, you will have choices. If your heart ultimately leads you on a path other than college, then listen. Only YOU know where you are headed.

TIP #29   Number Two Is Sometimes Number One.

TALE:
Big Jess, Big Love

I don't think there was a single A- on her transcript, just straight As across the board. The only reason she was salutatorian of our class was because Dan had taken just one extra honors class our freshman year. The grade point average may have selected him as valedictorian, but to everyone else in the class, "Big Jess" was everyone's number one.

Involved in *everything* on campus, Jessica became known as "Big Jess" when she sang a solo at an assembly in the spring of freshman year, and brought the house down. "That *girl* got some BIG lungs," At practice the next morning, Keisha announced "Big Jess" as the cheerleader of the week, and so it stuck.

Jess knew everyone's name in a class of 300. Big "GOOOD Mornings" and big hugs were given out everyday. Jess was a perfect cross between hometown beauty queen and high school nerd. She treated everyone equally, and that's what made her so special.

I don't know if Jess knew how every senior was rooting for her to be admitted to her first choice college, UCLA. She had been limited to applying to public schools in California, with the exception of a few private Christian colleges where she was eligible for large scholarships. UCLA had been her dream since sixth grade, and Bellflower High had not had an acceptance there for three years. When she was admitted, news spread throughout the campus, and students, teachers, administrators, and even

The college admission process calls on you to make your first real adult decision.

the maintenance staff stopped to give a hearty, "Congratulations." Just before spring break, Jessica's mom, Mama Leslee, sent in the deposit to UCLA, and she was officially a Bruin! As best friends, we would become cross-town rivals.

The final weekend in April, Big Jess attended Azusa Pacific University's "Cougar Pride" event as a guest of former BHS choir singer, Yuriko. While APU had offered a full tuition scholarship, the room and board was still more costly than UCLA. More than that, Jessica believed UCLA was the best choice for her future. Friday night, they hung out in the dorms and all of Yuriko's friends remembered Big Jess from a fall visit. The next day, they went to the spring festival, met other newly admitted students, and Jess was invited to join in with the choir that evening. Yuriko and Denise took Jess to the local "Doughnut Man" shop where at 1a.m. the line was around the corner. The three sat in the common room of the residence hall eating their Tiger Tail doughnuts until four o'clock in the morning chatting about family, faith, and their future. At Bellflower High, Big Jess had all the answers, but somehow here in the quiet city of Azusa, she had found more questions.

Sunday morning, APU's Dean led chapel and began by saying, "I woke up this morning and scrapped my talk, for God has a different message for one of you in this audience." Big Jess will never quite remember what the Dean spoke of, but she can still feel the warm tears drip down her cheeks. She went to bed just six hours earlier questioning her life, her decisions, her faith, and woke up to have all her answers revealed in his 15-minute talk.

At 2 p.m., Mama Leslee picked up her daughter and Big Jess waved good-bye to five of her new best friends. She hardly spoke a word on the fifty-minute drive home. What to do? What about the deposit? How will we be able to afford this? Can I do this? Leslee turned on the radio and let her daughter contemplate.

Whether it is your gut, your intuition, your god, or your higher power. Somewhere inside you know exactly what to do.

Just before her father and brother arrived home from volunteering at the church, Jessica came out of her room, stood in front of the television to meet her mother's eyes, and said, "I'm supposed to go to APU. That is where I'm supposed to be." Mama Leslee stood up to embrace her daughter and confidently replied, "Well, if that is what you want, we will find a way."

Big Jess had the strength of a goddess. She did not care what anyone said or thought about her decision, and I knew not to try and convince her otherwise. Once she made a decision and her family supported it, it was a done deal. There is much satisfaction in being able to say for the rest of her life that she was admitted to UCLA, but not nearly as much satisfaction as graduating from

Azusa Pacific University. APU will forever be the place where Big Jess felt Big Love.

TRUTH:

This process can play with your head. To the outside world, you may seem perfectly calm, cool, and collected, but I know this is cause for much anxiety and stress. The college admission process calls on you to make your first real adult decision. This is hard stuff for anyone, so do not beat yourself up if you are struggling to make a final choice. I encourage you to tune everything else out and listen to what is inside your heart and soul. Whether it is your gut, your intuition, your god, or your higher power. Somewhere inside you know exactly what to do. Allow yourself enough time to make a decision, even if you change your mind five times. Once you know (you'll know when you know), voice what that is and don't look back. Soon you can get on to enjoying your final weeks with family and friends.

TIP #30

Ivy League Dreams
Sometimes Do
Come True.

TALE:
To Whom Much Is Given, Much Is Required.

The coolness of this winter day seemed fitting for Janah's first rejection. I say "rejection" because that is what it felt like to her, but in reality, it was a deferral from her first-choice college. From the age of 8, Janah had two dreams: first, to go to the best college possible and second, to become the President of the United States (POTUS). She fought hard to get admitted to Walter Payton High School in Chicago, where she would compete academically as one of the few African American students on campus. Her flawless grades, more than 12 Advanced Placement and honors courses, and impressive test scores were just the icing on the cake. Janah was on the Debate team; was a school ambassador; was on the Mayor's Youth Council; and had started her own podcast, "The Bottom Line," interviewing peers on topics such as Black Lives Matter, the economic divide in Chicago, and the American Asian Movement. Janah was more than qualified for Georgetown, but on this day in December, for the first time, this overachiever's confidence was shaken and imposter syndrome began to set in.

It had been late September when she prepped for five interviews through the Chicago Scholars program. On deck were meetings with American, George Washington, Georgetown, Columbia, and Barnard. American University accepted her right on the spot with a generous scholarship offer. Money would play a role in her final decision, so Janah was beyond thrilled to know so early in the process that she was officially going to college.

With one month before the Nov. 1 deadline, Janah's interview with the Admissions Representative had solidified her decision to apply Early Action to Georgetown. Unlike Early Decision, the Early Action option meant that she could wait and receive her financial aid package and still make her final choice by the May 1 deadline.

For Little POTUS (my nickname for Janah) proximity to "The Hill" seemed a perfect fit, but it was Georgetown's commitment to its religious roots that impressed her most. The unexpected deferral letter felt awful, and so, Janah did what she knew best: she prayed about it. "I have fought the good fight, I have finished the race, I have kept the faith," 2 Timothy 4-7, became her mantra.

After taking a few days off in December from thinking about college, Janah got back to work on applications. Additional competitive universities included the University of Chicago, University of Virginia (UVA) and University of California, Berkeley. So far, the list of Ivy institutions included Harvard, Columbia, and (for its American history roots) the University of Pennsylvania — an obvious choice for Little POTUS. I had long suggested Cornell and Princeton, and after some research, she added both to the list.

While Janah had already written nearly 12 essays, each of the

Ivy institutions, U Chicago, and UVA had their own supplemental requirements. Without complaint, for the next two weeks, Janah chipped away at each application, day after day. With each application, her stories improved and her confidence grew. Little POTUS was not taking "No" for an answer.

By April 1, Janah had fallen in love with numerous colleges and received 10 letters of acceptance, three waitlist letters, and two deny letters. While Little POTUS was ecstatic about a "YES" from Georgetown, she needed to be sure it was the place for her.

In the end, it came down to four schools. Janah made real connections with scholarship finalists at UVA, but realized Charlottesville was not the place for her. The fast pace of New York City and the sisterhood she felt made Barnard College a top contender. She spent two days at Georgetown and loved it. Like her own home, Georgetown provided the comfort of the familiarity of Christianity; the backdrop of an urban city; and more students, like Janah, ready to take over "The Hill." Janah missed the official welcome weekend at Princeton, but a friend introduced her to students and professors and taught her about the eating clubs. The conversations were exhilarating but, at the same time, it wasn't lost on Janah that she was one of very few African American students on campus, which made Princeton equally comfortable and uncomfortable.

There were so many reasons to choose Georgetown, but in the end, Janah reflected on what she eloquently wrote in her applications. As a public school student from Chicago, Janah plainly stated, "I have exhausted my resources. I want to extend my inquiry and engagement on a national scale. I'm in search of an institution that will fill the gap of my resources and serve as the gateway to The Oval Office."

The discomfort of Princeton was exactly what she longed for. The hustle of an urban city like NYC or DC was a bit too familiar, while Princeton would push her out of her comfort zone. The gothic residential halls would now become home.

TRUTH:

I've said before that the college admission process is NOT for the faint of heart. It takes complete courage and bravery for any 17- or 18-year-old to put themselves out there, heart and soul, and await a life-changing decision.

Even the overachiever, and perhaps **especially** the overachieving student, has faced imposter syndrome. Every student I've worked with (and there have been thousands) gets to senior year, begins to doubt who they are, and questions their ability to get through this process. Seniors simply lose it and can become paralyzed in their tracks. It's heartbreaking to watch, but those who can push and persevere will ultimately reap the benefits. The fact that YOU are still reading this book to the bitter end tells me that you'll get through it, just like Janah did.

The real truth, however, is to hold on to your dream and let go of a specific result. What Janah is after is a happy future, a fulfilled life, and a career of service. She understood from a very young age that one way (not the **only** way) to get closer to her life's ambition was to get accepted and attend a top college in the United States. Janah's mission to find the "right" school was specific to her list of "must haves," "should haves," and "could haves." From the beginning, she learned from me that for every college on your list, you must have a reason. You must be able to answer the question, "Why, out of the 3,000 colleges you could choose from, THIS college?" It must be specific to that college.

Having visited her top four colleges, it became crystal clear which institution was perfect for the person she aspires to become, not necessarily the person she is today. For Janah, that place is Princeton University. Having had the honor of working with Janah, I know she is ready to take on the world.

Congratulations, Little POTUS. May you inspire others to dream the impossible.

CHAPTER 7:
Resources and Final Note

I'm not going to sugar coat this, if you are a dreamer AND doer looking to get admitted to top 100 colleges, the road is not easy, but if you are willing to put in the work, it is worth it. Over the last few years, our students (aka "Campers") have been admitted to their top choice schools every year. If you want to hear from successful students admitted to colleges that admit under 20%, scan the QR code in the resource section at the back of the book and listen to hear directly from: Janah (Episode 149-152), Julia (Episode 146-148), Sean (Episode 142), Curtis (Episode 122), Max (Episode 131), Celeste (Episode 140), Juliana (Episode 120), Emilie (Episode 93), Julio (Episode 134), Hannah S. (Episode 125), Osose (Episode 110), Ashley (Episode 112) and Jadir (Episode 127).

FINAL NOTE:

Congratulations! One thousand times, congratulations! You are headed exactly where you are meant to be. This is an exciting time in your life. Get your team of supporters, village of cheerleaders and community of believers and go celebrate!

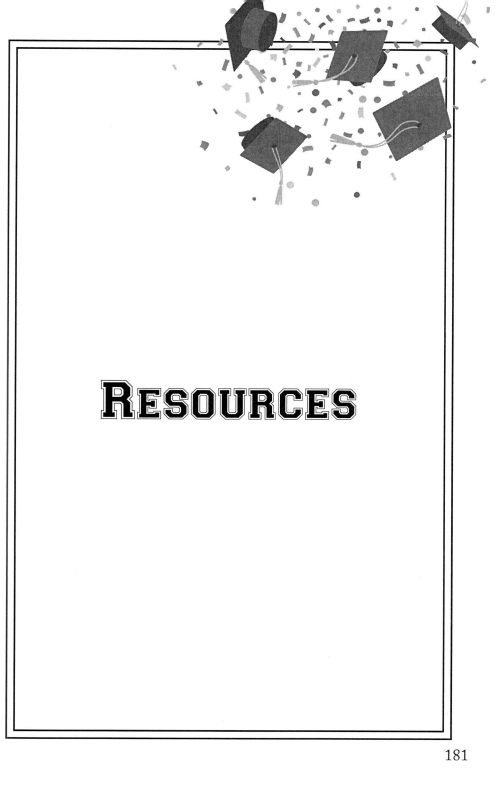

RESOURCES

I have been in this business for over 25 years, and I can't even keep up with all the resources available today. I have found the best thing to do is find someone you like and trust and go from there. Just like I had my mom and Mr. Vargas, every family deserves to have a guide, trust me, you do not (nor should you try) to do this alone.

OK, so below are a list of resources I give out to my campers and private clients!

DR. CYNTHIA COLON WEBSITE (AKA—MY WEBSITE)

Scan the QR code below, download some freebies, check out my blog, or schedule a free consultation. This is where you can also learn about our online and live courses and workshops. Dream College Academy is the comprehensive college counseling curriculum and College Essay Bootcamp is our signature course available as a digital course, virtual via Zoom, or live in person. When you join us, you become part of our family!!

DESTINATION YOUNIVERSITY PODCAST (AKA, MY PODCAST)

Go and listen to my very first guest, Lydia Franco, my mother. She gives every parent the inside scoop on the ONE word every parent should remove from their vocabulary! Also, at the end of each chapter I offer suggested podcasts to listen to to further your game on that topic!

 Scan this QR code with an iPhone or iPad to open the Apple Podcast app and start playing Episode 1 of my podcast!

If you're an Android or Pixel user, scan this QR code to open my podcast on the Google Podcasts app. *(Note: You may need to change your phone settings to enable QR scanning)*

Can't listen on the Apple or Google podcast apps? No Worries, just search Destination YOUniversity wherever you get your podcasts!

COLLEAGUES I KNOW AND TRUST:

Stephanie Hancock, "The Financial Aid Lady"
https://www.collegeaidworks.com/

Jocelyn Paonita Pearson, The Scholarship System
https://thescholarshipsystem.com/

Julia Byrd, Essay Coach
https://essay-coach.com/

DR. C'S GO-TOS

Below is a list of the books I read, podcasts I listen to and planners I use. Why am I giving you this list? Because I wish I knew then what I know today.

BOOKS:

Atomic Habits
7 Habits of a Highly Effective Teen
The Success Principles: How to get from where you are to where you want to be
Rich Dad, Poor Dad
The Seven Spiritual Laws of Success
Don't Forget To Write: For secondary grades
You Are A Badass

PODCASTS:

Destination YOUniversity
How I Built This
30 for 30
Real Estate Rookie
Running It Back

YOUTUBE:

Yoga with Adriene
TED
Let's Become Successful
Jimmy Kimmel Live
Clean & Delicious

PLANNERS/ JOURNALS:

Passion Planner
5-Minute Gratitude Journal
Oprah's The Life You Want Planner
All Journals from Journals Unlimited
My Hype Book

SUCCESS STORIES

SUCCESS STORIES: PARENTS

"It seemed that my daughter had all of the pieces to the puzzle, but we definitely needed help putting this jigsaw together. Dream College Academy (DCA, the online extension of this book) is where she discovered and learned to cultivate her passion project. The essay camp gave her the strategies to bring her ideas to the forefront. I'm glad that I took this leap of faith with Dr. Colon to help make her college dreams come true."

Cyntria R., Parent, Class of 2022
Chicago, IL
Janah, Princeton University, Class of 2026

"My daughter fought me a little at first, but finally agreed to do the 5-day College Essay BootCamp. She felt so accomplished and completed four essays and was able to use them and modify them for her numerous college applications with supplemental questions. Entering senior year of high school with 4 essays and a completed common app are priceless!"

Rebecca C., Parent Class of 2021
Mt. Kisco, NY
Julianna, Cornell University, Class of 2025

"My daughter was paralyzed in the college application process. Information was coming at her from everywhere, and she was overwhelmed. While I generally understood the college application process and my experiences were dated. I signed Bonnie up for Dream College Academy (the online extension of *Be Committed. Get Admitted!*) over spring break, which helped her learn how to research colleges that fit her goals and develop her application list. Then in the summer, Bonnie completed the College Essay BootCamp and came away with multiple essays to use for college and scholarship applications. Throughout the process, Dr. C demonstrated her genuine interest in Bonnie's success as she supported Bonnie's process and provided current and relevant insight that cleared away the confusion and illuminated the path. Bonnie was thrilled to be accepted at her dream school, where she is now excelling as she works towards a BFA in Dance."

Francie, Parent, Class of 2021
Placentia, CA
Bonnie, Rutgers Mason Gross School of The Arts, Class of 2025

"It was overwhelming to have two sons navigate the college admission process, one as a transfer student and the other as a high school senior. The anguish; however, turned into action quickly. Dr. Colón gave power to what essay topics highlighted their real selves. This process focused on finding their superpower and then writing about it with intention. They found topics that allowed them to amplify their personal stories in a real way. Her support launched their writing and gave them a roadmap to getting the essays done! In just 5 days, they took ownership of their application journey and felt empowered. I noticed that as the week went on and more essays were written the dread turned into accomplishment. I am grateful to have had Dr. Colón as a support for my boys."

Veronica R., Parent Class of 2020 & 2022
Half Moon Bay CA
Roman, USC Marshall School of Business, Class of 2024
Julio, USC Marshall School of Business, Class of 2026

"My wife and I were both first-generation college students who went on to have careers in higher education. We thought we knew everything about the current (competitive) college application process from our own experience, but we found Dr. Colón's insights were critical in preparing our children for their own successful application processes. More importantly, we read this book while our youngest daughter was in 8th grade, and she was able to benefit from applying the seven steps throughout her high school career. I attribute part of both of their successes in the college application process to the tools they had from this book."

Daniel S., Parent class of 2021 and 2018
Muncie, IN
Kelby, DePauw University, Class of 2022
Brooke, Ball State University, Class of 2025

"After researching online, I connected with Dr. Colón and my two sons began with Dream College Academy (the online extension of this book) in their junior year. As they learned the ins and outs about college admissions, I kept thinking to myself, we should have done DCA the second half of freshman year! If you are wanting more information than what your school guidance department provides, I implore you to learn through Dr. Colón's book, *Be Committed. Get Admitted!* and/or have your children take Dream College Academy when they are in grade 9 or 10."

Sarah P., Parent of twins Class of 2022
Brewster New York public schools
Sean, University of Virginia, Class of 2026
John, North Carolina State, Class of 2026

"The college admissions process was a daunting task until we were introduced to Dr. Cynthia Dr. Colón. My daughter participated in Dr. Colón's Dream College Academy (the online extension of *Be Committed. Get Admitted!*) and she also spent a week in the summer at College Essay Boot Camp. The essay really does set your student apart from others and having Dr. Colon and her expert team work with your student is a game changer. Start by reading this book, Dr. Colón is personable, relatable, and knowledgeable."

Karen H., Parent, Class of 2022
Costa Mesa, CA
Lauren, U Wisconsin Business School, Class of 2026

"Dr. Colón is full of knowledge, passion, energy, and heart. She genuinely cares for her students and helps them to explore their uniqueness and guides them to bring their stories to life. My oldest daughter came out of Essay BootCamp with countless essays, which she used for over 30 supplements. Soon after, we signed up her younger sister and the results were just as impressive. My girls are very different; nonetheless, they both gained insights to the essay and the application process. As a result, both of my girls were accepted into their top colleges with exceptional merit scholarships!!"

Denise B., Parent, Class of 2021 & 2023
Brooklyn, NY
Alexandra, Holy Cross, Class of 2025
Ava, Duke University, Class of 2027

"Always an achiever, Will struggled with promoting himself in college essays. Dr C's insight questions and essay writing methodology gave Will the tools he needed to identify his strengths, contributions and accomplishments then select and present them through stories that were uniquely his own. Rather than dreading the essay writing process, he became excited to see the progress made on each revision as his essays went from good to "Wow!" Whether your student has their sights set on an elite level school or is simply struggling with how to best present themselves in a college application, this is the place to start. Read this book, get your feet wet, and then take the classes! Best decision ever!!"

Leanne H., Parent Class of 2020
Huntington Beach, CA
Will, UCLA, Class of 2024

"Hi Dr. C - with your help my older daughter, Madeline, was accepted to Tulane and my younger son, Liam, was accepted into the University of Virginia! THANK YOU so much! I continue to recommend you here in Northern Virginia."

Eugene S., Parent, Class of 2021 & 2023
Northern Virginia
Madeline, Tulane, Class of 2025
Liam, University of Virginia, Class of 2027

"My son and I both read Colón's book, *Be Committed. Get Admitted!* With just that bit of information, her tips and strategies could have been enough. Left to his own devices I'm sure my son could have completed his applications and they would have been "good enough." Through her courses and individual counseling, Dr. Colón played a true coach role, pushing my son to be better than he even thought he could be. The result for him and myself is sheer elation and relief knowing he did the very best job he could have done. This process has changed him for the better and I can't wait to see the results."

Cynthia M., Parent, Class of 2023
Los Alamitos, CA
Colin, admitted to University of California, Santa Barbara, Purdue University, U Florida, Arizona State University

---

"Between the webinars offered by Dr. C, her Essay Bootcamp, listening to Dr. C's Destination YOUniversity podcasts, and reading her fantastic book *Be Committed. Get Admitted!*, our son was able to be committed, get his juices flowing and write essays to his long list of college applications. We have yet to meet another person with the knowledge, charisma, professionalism, caring attitude, and dedication that Dr. Colón offers to students and parents. Do not wait, get started early!"

Martha M., Parent, Class of 2023
Chula Vista, CA
Esteban, admitted to USC, Santa Clara University, Loyola Marymount University, U San Diego

SUCCESS STORIES: STUDENTS

"Dr. Colón truly believed in my college dreams and invested in my vision beyond college. With her help, I learned that college is not the end in and of itself; it's the means to the end—an avenue I must take on my journey toward my future aspirations and my purpose. Through Dream College Academy (the online extension of this book), College Essay BootCamp and private coaching with Dr. C, I learned to craft my activities, academic endeavors, curiosities, and passions into a cohesive narrative and persuasively articulated my vision of my future to each college. Dr. Colón provided admission secrets, essay writing tips, and gems for resumé building that I would not have received without her. However, I am most grateful that she encouraged me to daringly, unashamedly, and passionately proclaim my dreams and actively pursue them until they are realized."

Janah R. Class of 2022
Chicago, IL
Princeton, Class of 2026

"I am very grateful to Dr. C's College Essay Bootcamp. Working with Dr. C helped me to realize the potential I had to get into higher institutions. I was very stressed out at the time, being enrolled in multiple AP and dual enrollment courses, various clubs and teams on campus. As a result, college applications were at the end of my to do list. Fortunately, Dr. C helped me to hit the nail on the head and apply all of my experiences into beautiful essays."

Celeste N., Class of 2022
Lynwood, CA
Stanford, Class of 2026

"Dr. Colón was a blessing in my life, there seriously isn't any other person like her that is so dedicated and such an advocate for ALL of her students' success. My college journey was a bit different from others and went down the community college route, and I kept getting denied by all the schools I applied to. Dr. C understood my goals and provided the tools for success. Her knowledge for college admissions is above and beyond and I guarantee you can not find it anywhere else. After participating in Dream College Academy (the online extension of this book), I felt so prepared to begin my college admissions journey and sure enough I got accepted to UC Berkeley. Dr. C is the best, I just wish I found her sooner!"

Cosette R., Class of 2018
Silver Spring, MD
UC Berkeley, Class of 2023

"Dr. C's bootcamp was life-saving for me during the college process. I knew I was a motivated student but writing was never my forte, and I definitely needed some guidance. After five days with Dr. C and her awesome team, I left the camp with SEVEN essays and felt more confident in knowing how to write for college applications. Throughout her process I learned so much about myself and how to express that through my applications, as well. I am currently a sophomore at my dream university and I am confident that everything I learned in this camp helped me get to where I am now!"

Jules C., Class of 2021
Mt. Kisco, NY
Cornell University, Class of 2025

"Taking Dr. C's essay classes not only made me more confident in myself and my abilities but it also made me a better writer. Dr. C's class was instrumental in my success while applying to college, and I still find myself utilizing her tips and tricks in my day to day life during undergrad."

Ashley H., Class of 2021
UCLA, Class of 2025

"I was so stressed out when it came to applying for colleges, but Dr. C's workshops not only helped me get started on the right path, they also helped me get into multiple colleges, including my top school! Because of College Essay Bootcamp, I was able to organize and finalize the colleges I wanted to apply to. I was able to get all of my application documents in order with zero stress. Her essay writing camp let me get 8 different essays started, edited, and finalized in just 5 days. No matter what your college dreams include, get started! Dr. C is just the person to go to. Thank you, Dr. C!"

Bonnie Q., Class of 2021
Rutgers Mason Gross School of The Arts, Class of 2025

"With Dr. C's unmatched excellence, I created a remarkable set of essays with "me" written all over them. This project gave me the confidence and skillset to write about anything, no matter how "out there" they seemed. I left with eight nearly polished essays and completed my application season with twenty applications and over thirty essays. This renowned program has followed me from the very beginning of my application to my current work at the top college I'm attending. I am truly in debt to Dr. C as I've been under her incredible direction as a student and a mentor. Dr. C believes in all her Dreamers. I'm grateful to be one of those dreamers pursuing her dreams!"

Alexandra B., Class of 2021
Brooklyn, New York
College of the Holy Cross, Class of 2025

"Through her productive essay workshops, outstanding podcast episodes, and informational webinars, Dr. C helped me develop a clear plan for my college application. But most importantly, she helped me believe in myself and communicate my qualities, character, and life to admissions officers through extraordinary essay revisions and power words for my resume. I am extremely grateful to God to have met and worked with Dr. Cynthia Colon, because she has changed my life and set up my future for huge success."

Esteban M., Class of 2023
Chula Vista, CA
Esteban, admitted to USC, Santa Clara University, Loyola Marymount University, U San Diego

---

"Through Dr. Colón's incredible knowledge, passionate energy, and effective resources, my overbearing college admissions transformed into an enjoyable storytelling process. As a high schooler, it was difficult to write about my inner passions in a way that answered the essay prompts. But through Essay Bootcamp, I was able to write honest stories that made me so proud of the person I have become. Dr. Colón is one-of-a-kind. Her rare and gifted talent to help students find their own success is unmatched. I am so grateful to have chosen Dr. Colón as my college counselor and life adviser."

Jolene R., Class of 2023
Torrance, CA
Boston College, Class of 2027

"Dr C. is 1000% worth your while. My application would not even be half as strong without her guidance. She is an absolute expert in all things college and because of her expertise, she was able to simplify the process for me and almost make it easy to apply. Her feedback and instruction is invaluable and she harnesses the best version of me as an applicant. Don't wait to get started, open this book and start applying Dr. C's tips today!"

Matteo S., Class of 2023
Oakland, CA
Admitted to University of California at Santa Barbara, UC San Diego, Northeastern University

---

"After attending College Essay Bootcamp, I produced tons of essays which I was able to use to get many amazing acceptances and scholarships, all while being done before the holiday season. Dr. Colón and her team makes each and every day stress free all while being fun and enjoyable. Even if I was doubtful in my writing at first, the coaches never gave up on me and taught me to dig deeper and the words will come. In such a short, but valuable time, I found my inner voice and explored my confidence to truly sell myself in my applications."

Ava B., Class of 2023
Brooklyn, NY
Duke University, Class of 2027

"Over my time working with Dr. Colón, I have not only gotten to know her as a mentor but also as a friend. She is personable and insightful, she always surprises you with a college admission fact that you haven't heard before. She encourages you to do your best and congratulates you on even your smallest successes. I wouldn't have been able to do so well on my own, so thank you for guiding me through my college admissions."

Siena M., Class of 2023
Long Beach, CA
Admitted to, University of California at Berkeley, UC Santa Barbara, UC San Diego, U Washington

"Working through Dream College Academy helped me focus on the rigorous process I once found daunting. Dr. C guided me through what ideal applicants look like. She made me feel proud of what I had accomplished in high school and instilled the confidence to write intriguing essays. College Essay Bootcamp taught me that I can accomplish anything with clear goals. I can proudly say that Dr. Colon's programs have brought me to where I am today, with my acceptances into my dream schools."

Malik K., Class of 2023
Alexandria, VA
Admitted to, University of Virginia, William and Mary, Tulane University, Penn State

---

"Dr. C's guidance throughout my college application journey was outstanding. Her College Essay Bootcamp and private coaching taught me how to build my activities list and write my college essays in the most compelling way to convey my story and future aspirations to colleges. Dr. C also had many tips and pieces of advice for me to implement throughout the process, which gave me reassurance that my applications and essays were as strong as they could be. Not only was she amazing at giving college application advice, she was also one of my biggest cheerleaders. It was evident to me that Dr. C fully believed in my college dreams, and thus she made me more confident in myself too. Dr. C's college application guidance played such a significant role in helping me get accepted to multiple of my dream colleges."

Alexis C., Class of 2023
Placentia, CA
Admitted to, Yale, Cornell, U Pennsylvania, Northwestern, UCLA, Berkeley